Enrollment Management for the 21st Century
Institutional Goals, Accountability, and Fiscal Responsibility

Garlene Penn

ASHE-ERIC Higher Education Report Volume 26, Number 7

Prepared by

ERIC Clearinghouse on Higher Education
The George Washington University
URL: www.eriche.org

In cooperation with

Association for the Study
of Higher Education
URL: http://www.tiger.coe.missouri.edu/~ashe

Published by

Graduate School of Education and Human Development
The George Washington University
URL: www.gwu.edu

Adrianna J. Kezar, Series Editor

Cite as
Penn, Garlene. 1999. *Enrollment Management for the 21st Century: Institutional Goals, Accountability, and Fiscal Responsibility.* ASHE-ERIC Higher Education Report Volume 26, No. 7. Washington, D.C.: The George Washington University, Graduate School of Education and Human Development.

Library of Congress Catalog Card Number 99-61127
ISSN 0884-0040
ISBN 1-878380-87-7

Managing Editor: Lynne J. Scott
Manuscript Editor: Barbara M. Fishel
Cover Design by Michael David Brown, Inc., The Red Door Gallery, Rockport, ME

The ERIC Clearinghouse on Higher Education invites individuals to submit proposals for writing monographs for the *ASHE-ERIC Higher Education Report* series. Proposals must include:
1. A detailed manuscript proposal of not more than five pages.
2. A chapter-by-chapter outline.
3. A 75-word summary to be used by several review committees for the initial screening and rating of each proposal.
4. A vita and a writing sample.

ERIC Clearinghouse on Higher Education
Graduate School of Education and Human Development
The George Washington University
One Dupont Circle, Suite 630
Washington, DC 20036-1183

The mission of the ERIC system is to improve American education by increasing and facilitating the use of educational research and information on practice in the activities of learning, teaching, educational decision making, and research, wherever and whenever these activities take place.

This publication was prepared partially with funding from the Office of Educational Research and Improvement, U.S. Department of Education, under contract no. ED-99-00-0036. The opinions expressed in this report do not necessarily reflect the positions or policies of OERI or the Department.

EXECUTIVE SUMMARY

Public universities continue to experience significant change precipitated by a number of internal and external factors, among them constant turnover in administration, state and federal government regulations, and the general public's perception of higher education's value to society. Enrollment managers sit in a unique position to influence change, frequently high enough in the organization to have the president's ear. As an adviser to the president and governing boards, the enrollment manager must have excellent communication skills and extensive knowledge of policies and practices influencing the enrollment of students. The development, maintenance, and continuing enhancement of a conceptual framework for enrollment management and attention to external constituencies affecting enrollment are essential if the enrollment manager is to assist with positive institutional change.

Where Have We Come in Thirty Years?

Nearly three decades after the introduction of the term "enrollment management," individuals and organizations have developed a body of work describing various models of enrollment management. Enrollment management is an organizational concept and systematic set of activities whose purpose is to exert influence over student enrollments (Hossler, Bean, and Associates 1990, p. 5). It has four primary goals: to define the institution's nature and characteristics, and market the institution appropriately; to incorporate all relevant campus constituencies into marketing plans and activities; to make strategic decisions about the role and amount of financial aid for students and the institution; and to make appropriate commitments of human, fiscal, and technical resources to enrollment management (Dixon 1995, p. 7). Expanded and refined definitions of enrollment management have evolved over the past 10 years. In addition, computerized databases for recruitment and application, and telecounseling have provided tools enabling more efficient management of huge amounts of data about students (Bryant and Crockett 1993; Krotsen 1993).

Why Develop Tools for Enrollment Management?

Within the past two decades, two important situations have had significant impact on the business of higher education. The first was the decline in the number of young people graduating from high school who were eligible to attend a college or university. This decline signaled the start of increased competition among institutions for eligible potential students. After years of soaring enrollments with huge investments in physical plants to accommodate the new students, the number of people eligible and interested in attending college started a steep decline. It meant a scramble for the available students to fill classrooms and residence halls, with the result a buyer's market.

The second circumstance was the general public's erosion of trust in all types of public institutions (Hartle 1994), precipitated by a series of highly publicized events. Legislators responded by introducing legislation, calling for greater accountability, implementing performance-based funding, and mandating reports of specific statistical measures.

What Impact Does a Successful Enrollment Management Program Have?

Numerous surveys and studies over the course of 15 years show the impact of enrollment management systems on colleges and universities. Enrollment management programs vary widely in the way the concept is practiced, but the basic need to manage college enrollment from the point of initial contact through graduation has become increasingly apparent. Declining enrollments are second only to declining appropriations as the reason for colleges' and universities' financial problems. And enrollment management is an important factor in assisting institutions attain stated goals and remain financially viable.

What Can Enrollment Management Do for Administrators?

Institutions with a viable enrollment management program in place have reported success in meeting stated goals. A wide variation of the four original models is possible, with each model as distinctive as the institution itself. Although the division continues to be the most popular model, it does not guarantee success. Models range from a loose committee with representatives of student services involved to institutionwide committees with academic, fiscal, and student services areas involved. External factors play a huge part in the ultimate success of any enrollment management plan; some of them lead to more clearly stated goals, the development of measurement tools, and attention to the institution's mission. Other external factors may contribute to a complete breakdown in a once-viable management system. Internal factors also can lead to positive outcomes or to disruption. Loss of top executives when a plan is being implemented can halt the process and derail several years of planning and work.

Enrollment managers' concentration on data, quality service, cooperation, communication, and collaboration is important to institutional success. Those in the field must have broader formal and informal education. The chief enrollment officer must stay abreast of state and federal legislation, be able to discuss funding allocations, and know how to measure the general public's support for higher education. This professional needs background in computers, communications, marketing, research and analysis, personnel management, and fiscal concepts (Noel-Levitz 1996). The support generated for a comprehensive enrollment management program may be the result of the manager's ability to influence, communicate, persuade, lobby, and bargain with others. If a program is to be successful, the president or chief officer of the campus or system must not only endorse the program verbally, but also make sure it is funded. Therefore, the relationship of the chief enrollment officer to the president can be a critical element in a successful program.

The professional enrollment manager can, by using information databases and a combination of theory and practice, provide academic deans, the president, and fiscal officers with information about programs, the quality of students, demographic trends for graduates and potential students, attrition, and image. In an era when the number of potential students is beginning to rise again, less than 50 percent of those starting college actually graduate. Practices in awarding financial aid that may assist some students present financial problems for the institution and ethical concerns for the enrollment manager.

Institutions need to concentrate on the use of enrollment management tools, including predictive modeling, outcomes-based research on retention, programs, and activities, and evaluation of students' satisfaction to meet the needs of students, graduates, and society in general. Enrollment management changes the way colleges and universities approach the business of higher education. With appropriate planning and evaluation, institutionwide participation, well-prepared professionals, and adequate fiscal resources, enrollment management can help colleges and universities meet the challenges of the 21st century.

CONTENTS

FOREWORD

What exactly is enrollment management, and why should campuses embrace it? In his authoritative book on enrollment management, Hossler describes enrollment management as "an organizational concept and systematic set of activities with the purpose of exerting influence over student enrollments." *Enrollment Management for the 21st Century* examines this definition and many others. Yet the question remains, Why should universities consider adopting a new institutional practice, setting up yet another structure?

Higher education institutions have a long tradition of ignoring the enrollment process. Over the years, colleges and universities have closed, in part because they did not pay attention to their revenue stream or to the impact of enrollments. Campuses have also begun to realize that many different programs, services, and structures affect enrollment, yet these different influences are not coordinated. In turn, fluctuations in enrollment shape institutional processes and planning. New curricula may need to be developed because of changes in enrollment, housing or parking options may need to be changed based on the age of students, and program development may need to be altered by lower retention rates.

Current changes in the academy also make enrollment management a more significant concern. State mandates for accountability related to learning outcomes and student retention are tied to enrollment management. Campus systems of reporting patterns of student enrollments can indicate problems students are having and ultimately help to increase retention rates through active intervention instead of passive nonaction that lets struggling students fade away. Higher education institutions are recognizing that students have a better chance of succeeding and learning if various parts of the institution work together; enrollment management is a model of such collaborative decision making. Concerns about costs and maintaining access have made increased productivity and cost reduction a priority; effective enrollment management contributes to financial stability and maintaining lower costs per student. Marketing and admissions professionals work together to ensure enrollments fluctuate less. These changes in the academy provide opportunities for enrollment management. Innovations in technology offer more sophisticated systems for following students through the education pipeline. Institutions need to embrace these new technologies to maintain a strong financial base and to illustrate the institution's accountability.

Garlene Penn, director of enrollment services at The Ohio State University at Lima, examines trends, changes, and future directions in enrollment management. First, Penn reviews state and federal issues that affect the current enrollment management environment, including performance indicators, cost containment, greater access to higher education, decreased state funding, increased accountability, and federal regulations. She also examines changes in students and their families. Using models of enrollment management as a frame, Penn reviews enrollment management practices at public universities across the country. These cases illustrate the challenges and dilemmas facing enrollment managers and exemplary practices to solve them. They also assist in understanding that no one successful model exists. Although each institution adapts its practices to its culture, state policies, and individual leaders, the models presented and the literature reviewed outline key factors for any model: collaboration among campus units; a focus on a student's entire educational experience, from entry to graduation; the various functional aspects of enrollment management, including finances, promotion, planning, institutional research, and the curriculum; and communication to an institution's many publics. The last portion of the monograph details guiding principles for enrollment management professionals, including ways to evaluate an enrollment management model, the importance of communicating results, and how to face ethical dilemmas.

Two other ASHE-ERIC Higher Education Reports may also be of interest: *Pursuing Diversity: Recruiting College Minority Students* by Barbara Astone and Elsa Nuñez-Wormack and *College Choice: Understanding Student Enrollment Behavior* by Michael Paulsen. These monographs assist enrollment management professionals in diversifying student bodies and better understanding recruitment procedures that will result in enrolled students. These resources together should help to build an enrollment management model and a team that will meet the challenges of the 21st century.

Adrianna J. Kezar
Series Editor,
Assistant Professor of Higher Education, and
Director, ERIC Clearinghouse on Higher Education

INTRODUCTION

"Enrollment management" was the buzzword of student affairs professionals throughout the 1980s. Where are we today in relation to this theory or principle, nearly three decades after it first surfaced in the language of admissions and financial aid professionals at colleges and universities? We know that this concept has been implemented at colleges and universities across the country in nearly as many variations as there are components of enrollment management. Is enrollment management theoretical? Is it a practice? Is it a fad? What have we learned about institutions and about students' decisions regarding their attendance at various schools? Have we learned to use aspects of enrollment management to make our institutions better and our commitment to students stronger? In what ways?

Institutional researchers still study various aspects of enrollment management and report on enrollment projections and applications from such diverse fields as information systems, mathematics, marketing, student development, and education. A simple literature search generates a wide variety of articles, reports, and books for each key concept and the multiple layers of higher education. Numerous specialty organizations around the country cater to the enrollment manager, attempting to sell seminars, software, consulting services, application of marketing techniques, magazines, newsletters, and more. Weeklong conferences focus on aspects of the life of enrollment managers and the resources enabling them to do their jobs better. Student affairs professionals have always congregated to discuss concerns about students from middle school through college. Now mathematicians, engineers, computer specialists, and marketing/management organizations initiate partnerships with student affairs professionals that provide for broader discussion and the diverse use and interrelationships of multiple disciplines. Management information system staff assist in generating and analyzing the multitude of data collected from geodemographers, statisticians, government agencies, and the demographic and academic profiles of students. All this information enables enrollment managers to influence their institutions' enrollment programs. Facilities managers and institutional planners use the data collected and reported by enrollment managers to help determine academic and nonacademic programming and the use of buildings.

Some aspects of enrollment management have stimulated interest in strategic marketing, planning, and quality. The student affairs professional most concerned with enrollment management in the early 1980s was the director of admissions (Hossler 1984). Now the individual holding the position most concerned with the enrollment management equation is likely to have a significant background in statistics, computer applications, and marketing. The direct line of authority could be to the president, and the title could become, rather than just director of admissions, dean of admissions, dean of enrollment services, vice president, assistant to the provost, or even vice provost (Noel-Levitz 1996). Formerly, problems in enrollments were frequently defined as the need to recruit and admit an adequate number of students, with little concern for the aftereffects. Students who did not fit or were released by the institution for academic reasons were simply replaced with next year's new class. The focus of enrollments was on frontloading—the practice of oversubscribing a freshman class to account for attrition of sophomores and upper-level students. Now that definition incorporates size of the entering class, along with the mixture of current and prospective students by gender, race, academic preparation, geographic location, and any number of other characteristics (Dolence 1996). Officials consider students' satisfaction in selecting an institution, and retention of students to graduation. The physical and emotional environment, quality and quantity of teaching, faculty/student interaction, and effective use of institutional resources are all part of the equation for successful colleges and universities (Richter *n.d.*). The goal of enrollment now is to secure a tighter cadre of students that matches the institution so they stay enrolled and graduate. A high attrition rate is not desirable. In fact, low attrition/high retention is seen as a key indicator of institutional success. At its most simplistic, enrollment management is a way of organizing related functions to better serve prospective and current students while meeting institutional goals.

A review of the components of successful models and analyses of institutions that are practicing enrollment management will enable higher education administrators to determine the effectiveness of various models and methods of evaluation, and the personal and professional characteristics of successful managers to find those most applicable to their own situation (Dolence 1996). Thus, public university administrators around the country who have been identified through participation in the Noel-Levitz Enrollment Management Survey were interviewed, requesting responses in six primary areas (see Appendix A). First, each administrator was asked to define enrollment management for his or her own institution, identify the key elements, and provide a mission statement if available. Second, administrators were asked to list or diagram the structure under which enrollment management functions through an organizational chart or relationship description, and to explain which of four models—committee, coordinator, matrix, or division (Hossler 1984)—most nearly approximates the structure at their institution. Third, administrators were asked to describe how they evaluate their enrollment management program, key indicators of the program's success, and how this information is communicated across their campus. Fourth, they were asked about the longevity of the program and lessons learned as the structure took hold. Fifth, administrators were asked to discuss ethical concerns they might have, if any, in relation to practices of enrollment management. And sixth, they were asked to use their experience to provide advice to newcomers. This framework then enabled a discussion of enrollment management as it is practiced at major state-supported universities.

Although the internal locus of control for enrollment management remains primarily a function of student services (Noel-Levitz 1996), a number of significant external factors are important to consider first in determining how enrollment management fits into the overall picture of higher education institutions. The impact of federal regulations and financial support, and changes in the relationship between states and university systems must be considered before discussing how enrollment management models can benefit institutions of higher education.

Government Intervention, Public Opinion, and Public Universities

Public institutions are governed or influenced by a number of different constituencies. Most state institutions, for example, whether a single university or a complex system, normally have some type of governing board, whether it is called board of trustees, board of regents, or board of governors. This entity oversees the general administration of the institution or system and frequently evaluates the highest executive officer. Members of this board may be elected to office, but more frequently, board members are political appointees of the governor or some other appointing authority of the state. In addition, all states have a statewide board that either directs or recommends general policy for all public institutions. It may be coordinating or controlling (Wallenfeldt 1983), and it may report to the state legislative body through a variety of means, including committees, task forces, or specific, elected state legislators who represent the public interest in higher education.

The federal government is also concerned with education. It influences both national and state policy through several different departments, commissions, task forces, and cabinet posts. Other factors related to higher education are complicated by issues of accountability that have been raised by numerous publics, including the federal and state governments (Hartle 1994). With regard to accountability, an institution's success may appear to rest on such variables as time to graduation, retention rates, employers' opinions, and performance-based funding awards.

State issues

Access and accountability. The weight of public opinion on education has pushed legislators toward intervention in the business of education from early childhood through higher education. In different states, the emphasis has moved toward competency testing in elementary and secondary schools and toward performance funding for institutions of higher education. These states are struggling with issues of access to and quality of higher education, evaluation of faculty workload, and the relevancy of nontechnical degrees in the workplace (Cohen and King 1995). State coordinating boards find themselves in the position of attempting to meet the letter of the law as well as the needs of educational institutions in their state. All state boards, whether coordinating or controlling, are trying to walk a fine line between intruding into the operation of autonomous state-supported institutions and satisfying legislators who are heavily lobbied by angry constituents frustrated with the state of education across the country.

Dwindling financial and political support. Government financial and political support for higher education has drastically declined in the past 17 years (Breneman 1997) at the same time the public demands greater accountability. Less money is available to appropriate for any reason, and the government's priorities, particularly those of state governments, have shifted. Government entities prefer to exercise control over the industries they support, and they require definitive answers to hard questions about cost efficiency, productivity, and effectiveness. Government agencies and individual citizens are scrutinizing the cost of education and seriously attacking tuition costs. Financial allocations to higher education are under heavy scrutiny as states realign budgets to fund other priorities. Higher education institutions are forced to consider critical issues such as the cost of educating one student, graduation rates, and the rationale for continuing to offer remedial education (Levine 1997). The shifting relationship between public higher education and the government has put considerable pressure on institutions to find ways to be more accountable and to do more and better with less (Hartle 1994).

Today, public colleges and universities are in a fight for the state appropriations to which they feel they are entitled.

Today, public colleges and universities are in a fight for the state appropriations to which they feel they are entitled. Sweeping reforms in the welfare system that have moved welfare from the federal to the state arena place extraordinary pressure on state legislatures to provide job training and child care. In many states, the shift in allocations for higher education has caused increased competition between two-year schools, where many welfare recipients begin school for job training, and four-year and graduate educational institutions (Healy and Schmidt 1997), and some education officials, from both institutions and the government, have called this era the third phase in the historical evolution of public universities. State government support that has dwindled to a fraction of what was previously received has resulted in "the privatization of state schools" (Breneman 1997). Examples of lowered public support for higher education abound in the literature.

At the University of Michigan, for example, state support accounted for only 10 percent of total revenues and 18 percent of the 1997 academic budget. In Virginia, state support in 1995–96 accounted for 13 percent of total revenues and 21 percent of the academic division budget. In the early part of the 1990s, state support of higher education nationally dropped from 14 percent to 12.5 percent. In California, it went from 13.8 percent to 11.3 percent, in Minnesota from 19.9 percent to 17 percent, and in New York from 9.8 percent to 8.5 percent (Breneman 1997). Many university presidents have joked that, once state supported and then state assisted, their institutions now seem to be only state located.

Less support, more control. One might assume that with less state support, state influence over educational decision making would also become less. The reverse appears to be happening, however. In Virginia, for example, where the state provides 21 percent of the University of Virginia's revenues, the governance board comprises individuals appointed by the governor, increasingly an overtly political decision. The question arises then as to why the state, contributing roughly 20 percent of the institution's operating revenue, should control 100 percent of the governing body's makeup. In 1997, the governor of Kentucky separated the community colleges from the state university system and placed them under a separate governing board. In Maine, a state mandate requires the university to discontinue reliance on state funds and put into place early retirement policies, and the university is permitted to replace only 10 percent of those retiring. In California, the board mandated a reduction in the number of "special admits"—students in a particular admission category who appear to have an extremely low persistence rate.

In Ohio, Oregon, and Tennessee, proponents of the quality movement have instituted performance reviews of institutions, faculty, and programs—actions whose effect is unfunded mandates as schools struggle to come into state-legislated compliance. Frequently, a minimal allocation of funds—usually less than the cost of meeting the mandate—is their only reward. And they tend to generate incrementally unhealthy competition among schools that are both similar to and different from one another. Rather than making schools more efficient, the result is a scramble for the funds through any means possible, even if it means abandoning distinct missions. Despite the fact that many state budgets are in better shape than in the 1980s, most experts predict that higher education will never regain the share of funding it once received.

Such issues are prevalent in most states, and they affect the majority of public institutions. State issues are only a fraction of the external factors with which institutions must deal, however. The role of the federal government is becoming increasingly significant.

Federal issues

Aid, reform, and regulation. Postsecondary education is important to individuals and to the general welfare of the country. As such, the federal government has a significant role in promoting educational opportunity, and several developments in national education policy play a part in directing the actions of the government (Cohen and King 1995). For example, the change in financing higher education, noted earlier with regard to state appropriations, has a federal counterpart as Congress continues to struggle with a balanced budget. Some federal aid and sponsored research programs are bound to fall victim to any effort to reduce the deficit. Although many programs will not be phased out completely, the effect of reduction will create changes in institutional management of student aid, sponsored programs, and the like. Key congressional leaders have frequently called for educational reform or special commissions. One outlined for investigating rising tuition, for example, would determine whether the availability of student financial aid has caused higher tuition.

The increasingly heavy regulatory burden imposed by the federal government is easily illustrated by the regulations affecting financial aid through the U.S. Department of Education. In 1992, the regulations covered 7,000 sections of code, of which 555 mention the application process, 403 refer to other federal regulations, 27 deal with compliance, 159 provide definitions, and 152 spell out reporting requirements. In addition, the department issues a regular newsletter, *Dear Colleague,* to apprise financial aid directors of changes along the way (Hartle 1994, p. 15).

Coping with federal regulations affects all society. In the case of regulating higher education, it involves a fundamental tension between competing values. "Colleges, more than other social organizations, need autonomy and independence to fulfill their responsibility most effectively, whereas government needs accountability and control to ensure that taxpayer funds are well spent" (Hartle 1994, p. 15). The history of higher education in the United States is one of autonomy. This autonomy has provided for numerous examples of innovation and experimentation in higher education.

What contributes to greater federal regulation? Five factors appear to contribute to an increase in federal regulations affecting higher education. First, the necessity to regulate higher education like other enterprises is perhaps the recognition that higher education has become a "mature industry" (Levine 1997). Higher education is no longer automatically exempted from certain regulations.

Second, the government has a strong interest in protecting the consumer (Hartle 1994). Individuals and groups of society want and have available information about the quality and effectiveness of products they buy and use. Society determines what the measure of quality is, and industries are expected to conform. Thus, colleges and universities are now required to publish such figures as graduation rates, crime statistics, and expenditures for intercollegiate athletics. Individuals then make their own comparisons to determine quality and value. But while these indicators may be important and valuable for some societal purpose, they do not necessarily reflect the central mission of higher education—the development of intellect and creativity in ways that enable students and graduates to make intelligent choices and exercise leadership. These intangibles are not easily measured. So colleges use quantitative indicators such as completion rates and time to degree as substitutes, although such indicators may have little to do with quality of the product, the ultimate education of students, and their impact on society.

Third, the perception of abuse of public trust has caused the public to demand more regulations. Only a few colleges or universities have ever been involved in misconduct in research, abuse of student financial aid, scandals in intercollegiate athletic programs, or the reimbursement of indirect costs for a contract, but government officials are more willing to regulate all of higher education and less inclined to believe that educators really know what they are doing. The abuses of a few have created issues of compliance for the rest. The attempt to establish state postsecondary review entities is an example. SPREs would be designed to focus on serious problems of fraud and abuse in a state, and possibly to set statewide standards for graduation rates, withdrawal rates, and passing rates on licensure examinations. If implemented, SPREs would fix the minimum percentage for these standards (Hartle 1994, p. 18). Educators are concerned, however, that these minimum percentages would be too high or too low. If they are too high, the rates may interfere with schools' ability to serve nontraditional students, and if they are too low, the minimum standard become meaningless.

Fourth, federal regulations as enacted apply to institutions of higher education with regard to a number of other agencies. For example, the Office of Civil Rights is concerned with problems and policies involving racial harassment; NASA, NSF, and HHS deal with research involving animals and human subjects and with the reimbursement of indirect costs; and OSHA is involved with safety and environmental concerns (Hartle 1994, p. 20). Moreover, higher education institutions must also comply with some legislation covering various other agencies, for example, age discrimination in the form of mandatory retirement, particularly as it relates to faculty (Cohen and King 1995).

Fifth, total federal funds allocated to higher education is not a small amount. Even though discretionary funds such as Pell grants have not grown, the federal government in 1995 provided an estimated $30 billion through grants and increased student loans and another $15 billion in federal research funds to colleges and universities—a total of $45 billion that must be accounted for. Federal aid is a double-edged sword. The government uses it as leverage to push institutions and the higher education industry in certain policy directions. The upshot of this federal assistance, regardless of the type or distribution, is more intrusive regulations for higher education.

Regulation does not come cheap! Government regulations pose a twofold burden for higher education institutions. First, regulation is not cheap. Compliance is costly, requiring specialized staff and information systems, but noncompliance can be even more costly. Schools have been known to increase tuition and/or reduce expenditures to meet the requirements.

Second, regulations tend to interfere with academic independence and autonomy. This aspect of higher education is essential to preserve the diversity of higher education and the wide range of opportunities available to all students. Independence and autonomy encourage educational innovation and ensure academic freedom. Yet as government support has risen, the independence of higher education institutions has been hampered. The government wants to ensure that colleges and universities effectively and efficiently serve the public interest. A proper balance must be maintained to allow for autonomy and accountability (Hartle 1994).

The public perception. Some similarities can be seen between the status of higher education and the status of health care in this country. The public perceives that doctors and hospitals are the main reason for skyrocketing costs in health care and believes they are cheating the public. College and university faculty have been perceived to be guilty of the same actions; hence, questions arise about teaching load, leaves of absence, tenure, and a variety of other related academic matters. The government has attempted to force health care in line using federal regulation, and it now is moving toward a similar agenda for higher education. The media fuel this movement by writing horror stories about fraud in financial aid, apparently escalating tuition costs, and high salaries for senior faculty and administrators. Yet expenses for higher education are small in comparison with other programs in the federal budget or in individual and family budgets. The cost of higher education is limited and an issue that affects only a small fraction of the population and only for the duration of attendance. For personal budgets, higher education is a relatively short-term problem when compared with other items, such as health care (Baum 1994).

Yet, like health care, higher education faces a crisis of confidence that challenges its fundamental mission, values, and performance. The appeal of higher education will never be universal. Some people will value it more than others, which can be seen in the issue of willingness to pay—as compared with ability to pay. Parents display a growing unwillingness to pay for college for their children, causing a shift in the burden of educational cost to students through increased indebtedness, which will affect their economic power after graduation. Higher education administrators must learn the lesson of the health care debate and be prepared to work to cut the cost of operations and realign priorities so that educators, potential students, and society in general will value higher education.

One predictable institutional response to lower state and federal funding is to increase tuition (Cohen and King 1995, p. 46). That trend in the early 1990s led to a 12 percent jump in average annual tuition at public four-year institutions. Tuition bills are a major concern for students and their families. Politicians and citizens at large continue to demand that colleges and university tighten their belts, so tuition increases to make up for the loss of other revenue certainly will not be tolerated for long. Moreover, excessive increases in tuition would unnecessarily limit access to education for the have-nots, the very individuals who need public education the most. A few institutions have cut tuition in an attempt to halt dropouts for financial reasons (Speck 1996). But most colleges view reductions as risky for the budget or an outright giveaway to the rich. Some states have introduced bills to offer tax benefits for families who invest in college tuition beginning when their children are young and continuing to adolescence. Some are prepayment plans, some are tax breaks for the family and for the student. The federal government recently introduced tax credits for college tuition for the first two years of enrollment.

Many public institutions have begun to invest heavily in fundraising, much as private institutions did in the past. It is not realistic, however, to expect to replace all lost tuition revenues with private contributions. Most donors are not so eager to have their contributions go toward an institution's general operations; many choose to restrict their funds to specific projects (Breneman 1997).

Demographic Implications for Higher Education

The implications of federal and state support as it affects institutions of higher education must also be weighed with demographic factors such as the size and ethnic makeup of potential college classes, the probable location of those students, and the professions and jobs for which they must be prepared. Planning on the basis of demographic knowledge is essential if higher education is to become less reactive and more productive.

Enrollment projections by the U.S. Department of Education showed a higher percentage of students enrolled in higher education in 1992 than in 1982, despite trends that might indicate lower enrollments (Dixon 1995). Shifts in enrollment point to changes in the composition of the student body. More graduate students are enrolled than in the previous decades, and the percentage of students enrolled in two-year colleges has increased. Moreover, the so-called nontraditional populations—ethnic minorities, older students, and women—have greater needs (Dixon 1995). And colleges and universities have come to depend on these populations during the past two decades of a smaller traditional-age student body.

Age, graduation, and locale

Despite the availability of demographic data and the experiences of elementary and secondary schools, institutions of higher education have been weak in planning for future generations of students. In the face of predictions of severe decline, 42 percent of presidents of institutions in one survey expected the institution's enrollments to increase, while another 32 percent expected enrollments to remain steady

(Breneman 1983b). In the late 1970s, demographers became alarmed as they watched the decline in the number of eligible college-age persons. Undergraduate enrollments increased rapidly during the 1970s, reaching a peak of 2.3 million in 1979, then bottomed out in 1994 (Snyder and Hoffman 1995). Projections for 1992 through 2009 estimate that the peak in enrollments in undergraduate institutions will be higher in 2008 and 2009 than in 1979, and then will be followed by another leveling off (Western Interstate 1993). Differences will, however, exist across regions and states. By 2008, for example, all but five states will have recovered from the loss of graduating high school students, but some recoveries will be much higher. Enrollments in Nevada are projected to increase 212 percent over the 1979 figure, while those in Iowa are projected to be up only 1 percent (Western Interstate 1993, p. 16). Thirteen of the states that will have significant increases are in the western part of the country. Graduates of public high schools are expected to increase 3 percent, while graduates of private schools will show erratic spurts of growth and loss before 2004, when the number will level off at about an 8 percent increase over 1979 (Western Interstate 1993).

Regardless of the state or district where they live, more young adults will be graduating from high schools in the first decade of the 21st century. By 1995, the baby boomlet phenomenon began to show this projected increase in potential college students. The number of high school graduates stopped dropping and began an upward trend, which is predicted to peak in the first decade of the new century at around 3.3 million. While projections from the mid-1980s seem to indicate a drop in higher education enrollments until 1998 (Snyder 1987), a higher percentage of students graduating from high school and pursuing further education may account for some early increases in enrollment. Further, the baby boomer student will present additional opportunities for colleges as these nontraditional students reenter college to use pension and retirement dollars for personal and intellectual challenge (Trachtenberg 1997).

Colleges and universities have several opportunities as the number of traditional-age students increases over the next 10 to 13 years (Edmondson 1997). When the number of high school graduates dropped in the 1980s, most institutions coped with the reduction by increasing their percentages of older and part-time students and by redefining what a college student is (Edmondson 1997). A transformation in higher education now would target four specific markets to maintain institutional viability: 18- to 24-year-olds (the baby boomlet), who have changed the ratio of minority group members to the majority population from 1 in 4 to 1 in 3; 25- to 34-year-olds; 35- to 54-year-olds (the baby boomers); and the 55-and-over group. The Census Bureau predicts growth in the under-18 group (the traditional age for college recruitment), 18- to 24-year-olds, 35- to 54-year-olds, and the 55-and-over group through 2010, with slow but steady growth in the under-18 group after then (Edmondson 1997, p. 26).

Three other markets will help institutions remain viable into the next century if they use the information to modify themselves so as to attract and retain these lifelong learners (Edmondson 1997, pp. 29–30). First, more individuals aged 25 to 34 will continue to enroll in institutions of higher education for training, although probably only part time. The increasing cost of full-time enrollment has forced many individuals to seek education part time while working full time. It is ever more widely recognized that the difference in lifetime earnings can be attributed to advanced education, and with that recognition comes the necessity for institutions of higher education to accommodate individuals with part-time programs and a variety of ways to achieve their individual goals.

Second, baby boomers are constantly in school. Retraining is a requirement for many careers today, offering greater opportunities for continuing education at colleges and universities. Third, the over-55 crowd contains many individuals who have finished one career and may be looking for additional education or to continue interrupted education. They represent an opportunity for liberal arts and leisure-type educational programs. And the National Center for Education Statistics estimates the number of college graduates will increase 8 percent by 2010, providing yet another opportunity: a continuous market of individuals for further education and retraining (Edmondson 1997, p. 30).

Challenges for society
Other societal changes have created differences in the population of newly graduating high school students. The family unit has changed drastically, with more single-parent households and most mothers working outside the home, even in

two-parent families. One of the major factors in this transformation will be the increasing gap between the haves and the have-nots (Edmondson 1997, p. 28), and it is not only a cultural and racial/ethnic consideration, but also an educational issue. Information from the Census Bureau demonstrates the difference between cultures in relation to two-family homes and in educational background compared with lifetime income. Twenty-three percent of children lived in poverty in 1995, up from 16 percent in 1977—an increase of 7 percentage points in 18 years (p. 28). These poorest children (the have-nots) will come to higher education having had the least access to technology in their classrooms and possibly the least opportunity to reach beyond their family situation.

For years, demographers have predicted changing patterns of diversity in the baby boomlet group (traditional-age students) (Edmondson 1997, p. 28). Baby boomers brought a 1 to 4 ratio of minority group members to the majority population. The boomlet group has changed that ratio to 1 to 3. This issue of diversity will also be demonstrated by more multiracial children crossing several ethnic and racial cultures.

Age, ethnic and racial diversity, educational level of family members, stability of the family, and poverty will challenge colleges and universities as they target this population for entry into their institutions and ultimately into the professions. Overall, demographic trends for the next dozen years present a positive picture, but colleges and universities must manage resources well and not be afraid of bold changes in methods of delivery and programming (Edmondson 1997).

... colleges and universities must manage resources well and not be afraid of bold changes in methods of delivery and programming.

ENROLLMENT MANAGEMENT

Many colleges and universities currently use the term "enrollment management." It is a method of using more ideas and talent to better manage the institution in which administrators, faculty, staff, and students have a stake. At its best, enrollment management creates a highly interactive team of committed staff and faculty that uses established principles of planning, implementation, evaluation, and revision to ensure the institution's constant and consistent success in meeting its educational commitments to students while remaining accountable to its many publics. Enrollment management is a mature concept, one that now deserves high visibility (Dixon 1995, p. 7).

The need to manage college enrollment from the point of initial contact through graduation has become increasingly apparent. It has taken on more importance as higher education professionals begin to examine the serious financial problems confronting most colleges and universities today. Enrollment managers must have access to information about federal and state sources of funding, and must understand demographic factors to be able to appropriately assist their presidents face the challenges before them. A survey for the National Association of College and University Business Officers (Shafer and Coate 1992) found that declining enrollment was second only to declining appropriations as the reason for financial problems. Many respondents to the survey saw stable or increased enrollment as the primary reason for institutional stability.

The goals of enrollment management provide an underpinning for stable enrollment. It is an organizational concept and a systematic set of activities. Its purpose is to "exert more influence over student enrollments. . . . It is organized by strategic planning and supported by institutional research. . . . It concerns student college choice, transition to college, student attrition and retention, and student outcomes" (Hossler, Bean, and Associates 1990, p. 5). The bottom line is to find, enroll, and retain sufficient numbers and kinds of students who are desired by the institution.

Enrollment management has four goals (Dixon 1995): (1) defining the institution's nature and characteristics through the use of objective and subjective methods and marketing them both appropriately and aggressively; (2) bringing all relevant campus parties together in the marketing plans and activities around the core institutional goals; (3) making strategic decisions about the role and amount of financial aid needed to bring and retain the desired student body;

and (4) making substantial commitments to people, money, and technology to enable plans to be implemented (p. 7).

Definitions from the Literature

An early definition of enrollment management saw it as a *concept* and a process that "leads to issues of mission and goals clarification and budgetary decision making" (Kemerer, Baldridge, and Green 1982, p. 21). It was deemed an assertive approach that would ensure a steady supply of qualified students, with the intended outcome being maintenance of institutional viability (Kemerer, Baldridge, and Green 1982). An expansion of this definition clarified both primary functions and offices involved as well as related services affecting enrollment efforts (Hossler 1984). Those primary offices and functions included marketing, recruitment and admissions, pricing, and financial aid. Secondary or related areas heavily influenced by enrollment management plans included academic advising, institutional research, orientation, retention, and traditional student services. Another definition, using Hossler's, emphasized integration and coordination of offices and activities having direct influence on recruitment and maintenance of students (Pollock 1987b).

A UCLA institutional planner and researcher defined enrollment management as a "comprehensive approach requiring integration of related functions to achieve optimum recruitment, retention, and graduation of students" (Dolence 1988, p. 14), recommending that such an approach include strong links with academic programs, institution-wide recruitment and retention, and a strong orientation toward operations. The enrollment management *process* involves the entire campus (Hossler 1984).

Enrollment management has been called a "rational model grounded in fairly expansively documented theory" (Graff 1986), "a gestalt" (Greene 1987), "an umbrella term" (Kemerer 1984–85), and "a plan addressing administrative structure" (Hossler 1986; Kreutner and Godfrey 1980–81). The common thread through all definitions of enrollment management is that it is a coordinated, institution-wide effort. It involves a wide variety of areas within the institution. In addition to admissions, marketing, and financial aid, functions such as academic advising, retention, academic planning, career services, alumni relations, and development are integral to successful enrollment management. Enrollment management incorporates all the components of marketing, teaching, evaluation, and research into a system that focuses on the institution in holistic terms (Hossler 1986). Like strategic planning, the practice of enrollment management emerges from the institution's mission statement. One of its key elements is a clarification of institutional mission and long-range planning (Kemerer 1984–85). A successful enrollment management program changes the way the institution perceives its constituencies, confronts challenges, exploits opportunities, and manages resources (Dolence 1988). It modifies the institutional decision-making process.

Numerous researchers through the past two decades have defined, modified definitions, and redefined enrollment management. An integrated systems approach, it cuts across several administrative areas and traditional boundaries (Hossler 1986). Five key variables lead to the success of enrollment management: product, data and information, communication, management, and climate (Ingersoll 1988). Further clarification of each key variable shows remarkable similarity to earlier definitions (see Kemerer 1984–85; Kemerer, Baldridge, and Green 1982; Kreutner and Godfrey 1980–81).

Four Models of Enrollment Management
Four fairly distinct models were articulated in 1982 from the early work of Kemerer, Baldridge, and Green. Moving from loosest in terms of organizational structure and impact to tightest, they are (1) Enrollment Management Committee, (2) Coordinator, (3) Matrix, and (4) Division. Table 1 is an adaptation of the four enrollment management models as envisioned by Hossler (1986, p. 41).

TABLE 1

Models of Enrollment Management

Model	Degree of Restructuring Necessary	Authority
Committee	Low	Influence
Coordinator	Some	Networks
Matrix	Moderate	Cooperation
Division	High	Direct

The following definitions are useful in understanding the timing and implementation of these four models:

1. The *enrollment management committee* is usually the first response to problems related to enrollment. It focuses on marketing and admissions, or student retention, or takes a holistic view of student enrollment. It typically involves a few key faculty members, middle-management administrators, and perhaps a senior officer. It is a good starting vehicle, but the committee has no real authority and little chance at making a significant impact.

2. An *enrollment management coordinator* is typically a middle-level administrator with assigned responsibilities to coordinate and monitor the institution's enrollment management activities, primarily admissions and financial aid. The personal influence of the individual holding this type of position is the only indicator of impact. The position has little influence on policy and procedures, and thus the coordinator is held accountable for monitoring activities.

3. An *enrollment management matrix* links administrators directly responsible for enrollment of students with one senior-level administrator ultimately responsible for the process. This model provides a greater possibility of direct impact on policy and procedures but is still fairly dependent on the senior administrator's communication skills and influence.

4. The *enrollment management division* provides the most centralized systems approach. All major offices within the institution report to a single senior-level administrator, usually with a direct link to the provost or president. Although this approach represents the most radical reorganization, it provides the most responsive system to significant change in the process.

An overview with commentary on the timing of each model and its relative impact on institutional change (Dixon 1995) notes that the enrollment management committee is essentially a communication vehicle to inform various individuals and offices on campus about the institution's needs. A coordinator is only as effective as the influence of the individual in that post. In some situations, the approach is very effective; in others, the lack of direct authority to make change is damaging. The matrix does not require reshuffling administrative units but depends on more or less voluntary cooperation among affected offices, usually student services. The division is the most centralized model and requires some significant administrative changes to merge units affecting enrollment into a cohesive group overseen by a senior administrator (p. 8).

Links between Enrollment Management and Other Institutional Programs

An enrollment management program should include strong links with, at a minimum, academic programming, institution-wide recruitment and retention programs, admissions, financial aid, advising, institutional research, and alumni relations—as well as a variety of other seemingly unrelated operations (Dolence 1988). Typically, institutions begin by marketing their admissions process and gradually move along the continuum until reaching the most sophisticated approach that involves multiple constituencies of the campus.

Most approaches to enrollment management move along a continuum, from fewest activities or offices involved to a wide range of affected areas. In fact, the same institution may modify the model a number of times to make it more efficient for its particular campus. One progression that many institutions could take in the quest for enrollment management is illustrated in table 2 (Hossler 1986). The key elements at the far right of the continuum appear to be related in ways that can significantly influence student enrollment.

Other research (Pollock 1987b) sought to discover the prevalence of organizational management in colleges and universities in the mid-1980s. Roughly 60 percent of colleges and universities surveyed had instituted some form of enrollment management, most of them established within a three-year period during the mid-1980s. Moreover, three-quarters of the remaining schools in the survey anticipated instituting enrollment management by the early 1990s.

Since the late 1980s, literature pertaining to enrollment management has been rich in terms of marketing, leveraging financial aid, retention programs, and new, better, and faster technologies to enhance the recruitment pool. A book containing several case studies of successful enrollment management programs focuses primarily on the connection be-

TABLE 2

The Enrollment Management Continuum

Admissions Management	→	*Enrollment Management*
Marketing	Marketing and choice research	Strategic planning
Recruitment	Recruitment	Student services
	Financial aid	Institutional research and evaluation
		Marketing
		Recruitment
		Financial aid
		Academic advising and course placement
		Orientation
		Student retention programs
		Learning assistance
		Career planning and placement

Source: Taken from Hossler 1986 and modified.

tween admissions and financial aid (Dixon 1995), and although these two aspects are important components, clearly many institutions do not seem to have moved beyond the admissions/marketing mode of operation—yet they call it enrollment management.

Several books, written in cooperation with the American Association of Collegiate Registrars and Admissions Officers (Dolence 1993, 1996), discuss strategic enrollment management and highlight case studies of successfully implemented systems.

In the strictest sense, enrollment management is about the number and mix of students enrolled at any institution. But in the broader context, enrollment management is also about the people, the systems, the curriculum, the environment, and the attitudes of everyone involved in providing higher education. Complicated models for projecting enrollment derived from mathematical theory can provide tools to better prepare institutions for the realities of enrollment trends. A projection model, however, does nothing to enhance the environment of the student who is recruited, provided financial aid, registered in classes, tested, passed, presumably educated, and, one hopes, graduated from a higher education institution.

Does an Ideal System Exist?

If an ideal enrollment management system existed, it would probably incorporate a long list of units and individuals. The Noel-Levitz annual enrollment management survey asks respondents to indicate the functional areas (of a list of 15) for which the chief enrollment officer at their institution has direct administrative or supervisory responsibility. The list includes recruitment, admissions, financial aid, orientation, institutional research, public relations, student retention, registration, academic advising, learning assistance/academic support, career planning and placement, counseling, promotional publications, graduation, and alumni. In the 1995 survey, no institution listed all 15 areas (Noel-Levitz 1996). In fact, only 93.3 percent of respondents listed recruitment and 96.2 percent admissions as areas of responsibility for the chief enrollment officer (p. 70). "There is no ideal enrollment management system; there is only the application of the systems theory to influencing student enrollments in the unique situation that every campus represents" (Hossler and Kemerer 1986, p. 10). Core components or key elements form the basis for all enrollment management systems. Interrelationships between certain offices and functions in any institution—such as admissions and financial aid; admissions, orientation, and advising; market research and research on student attrition—seem to directly impact student enrollment.

Implicit (but not articulated) in any model is the importance of attrition among students, research on retention, and student outcomes. These factors have more to do with the academic environment over which enrollment managers exercise no direct influence. And, in most cases, it is not feasible to believe that faculty development or academic planning would be placed directly within such a student service–driven system. It is more likely that many of the academic functions will be aligned with the institution's teaching mission. They also, however, reside in a central

If an ideal enrollment management system existed, it would probably incorporate a long list of units and individuals.

theory that revolves around students' interests, needs, and learning styles as well as overall retention planning in some less formal, but highly committed, manner.

No one model of enrollment management applies to every institution; in fact, numerous case studies of institutions' practices illustrate various approaches to enrollment management. Rather than a single applicable model, colleges and universities demonstrate a broad range of possibilities serving individual institutions as well as complex university systems.

STUDIES OF ENROLLMENT MANAGEMENT IN THE 1990s

Nearly three decades after first use of the term "enrollment management," the literature contains numerous references to various aspects of successful enrollment management. The techniques have been learned and the right technological tools designed to carry out enrollment management for the next century.

Huddleston

Thomas Huddleston (University of Central Florida) conducted an enrollment management organizational survey of public and private institutions in 1996.* He asked five primary questions of the 385 institutions surveyed:

1. What were the reasons for the configuration of a new organizational model?
2. What were the results of having a new organizational model?
3. Do you believe your organizational model can be further improved?
4. Has the new enrollment structure met your expectations?
5. To what area does the enrollment management unit report?

The results, published in *College and University Journal,* tend to confirm much of what we already know about enrollment management and change some impressions of the earliest models. The response rate was 58.7 percent, with 37 percent of responses from public institutions and the balance from private institutions. Early reports demonstrated that enrollment management was more prevalent in private institutions, and that statement apparently is still true.

Some similarities apparently exist between private and public institutions that have been organized into an enrollment management model. For example, both types of institutions listed "increase student enrollment" as their first priority for the organizational configuration. Both types of institutions indicated an increase in student enrollments as one of their top two perceived benefits achieved as a result of the new model. (Public institutions listed "improve the

---

*Thomas Huddleston 1997, personal communication. The rest of the information in this subsection came from the same source.

efficiency of the units within the model" as the top benefit.) Both types of institutions view the model as dynamic, overwhelmingly opting for continuous improvement. Both types of institutions call for greater involvement from diverse campus groups, inclusion of academic support and assessment functions, the need for resources to allow strategic planning, and a customer-service, student-centered orientation.

Huddleston also found some differences between private and public institutions, however, in the actual organizational structure. At 51 percent of public institutions, the enrollment management unit reports to academic affairs, compared with only 20 percent of private institutions. Yet at more than 60 percent of private institutions, the enrollment management unit reports directly to the president, which was not even listed for public institutions. Undergraduate admissions is the one office represented in virtually all institutional arrangements, with financial aid and retention showing up as second or third.

Although four models of enrollment management are generally noted in every publication on the subject, most practitioners acknowledge that almost as many ways exist to organize for enrollment management as institutions practicing it. Huddleston's survey demonstrates this point again. Beyond one or two pivotal offices, the configuration of enrollment management is as individual as the institution itself.

NCEM

Each August, the National Center for Enrollment Management publishes the results of its survey from the previous fall, which looks at admissions policies and procedures, conversion and yield rates, the inquiry pool, recruiting and financial aid strategies and planning, organizational structure, budgeting, and staffing patterns (Noel-Levitz 1996).* The 1995 survey of four-year colleges and universities reported data from 438 institutions. Public institutions reported that the chief enrollment officer is responsible to the chief academic affairs officer or chief student affairs officer, very similar to the results Huddleston reported in his 1996 survey. The single most common title for the chief enrollment officer was still director of admissions at both public and private institutions.

The first year the survey asked for line of authority and areas of responsibility was 1992. It is interesting that since

*NCEM first published the information in 1992 for academic year 1991–92.

this area was first surveyed, responsibilities of chief enrollment officers have gradually increased toward a more integrated system, particularly at public institutions. Although
more than 90 percent of all institutions reported recruitment
and admissions as integral to their model of enrollment management, enrollment officers at public institutions appear
more likely to be responsible for registration and orientation
than their counterparts from private institutions (Noel-Levitz
1996, p. 24). Financial aid is a functional area of responsibility for at least one-half of all chief enrollment officers. Nearly
60 percent of all institutions reported a standing institution-
wide committee related to goals for enrollment, almost
equally prevalent at both public and private institutions. Although the importance of institution-wide commitment has
been emphasized, through some mechanism (such as a
standing committee) that would bring together the greatest
number of functional areas possible to plan strategically for
enrollment at an institution (Hossler 1984), at least 40 percent
of institutions practicing enrollment management have no
such mechanism (Noel-Levitz 1996, p. 70).

Dolence
Strategic Enrollment Management: Cases from the Field
(Dolence 1996) provides examples of strategic enrollment
management from a range of institutions, including graduate
programs, private universities, a community college, and a
number of large public universities. Some of the models are
long-standing and have been modified over the past decade,
and several are too new to evaluate meaningfully. None of
the institutions are configured alike, beyond a core of admissions and recruitment. The state of strategic enrollment management is in "constant flux," but Dolence at various times
has enumerated a "basic" model that would include admissions and recruitment, financial aid, registration, and retention. Through the case studies, he shows successful enrollment management structures, whether in academic affairs or
student affairs. The single most important consideration is
the availability and commitment of strong institutional support at the highest possible level.

ENROLLMENT MANAGEMENT AT MAJOR PUBLIC UNIVERSITIES

Large public universities have the advantage of name recognition, extensive research bases, a large faculty representing numerous specialties, and multiple programs to offer interested students. They also have the disadvantage of being extraordinarily large, which could mean the organization is slow to respond to specific needs because of a complex administrative structure or widely dispersed facilities and personnel.

Public institutions also have state mandates to maintain the level of student costs despite lower levels of public tax support, student grants, and other income. Frequently tied into student costs is the issue of access—the presumed right of every person to a publicly supported education. Yet costs accelerate at the same rate for the public sector as the private sector. Some of these costs include an increasing number of personnel to handle complex academic, information, and human systems, aging buildings long patched up with inexpensive solutions that no longer work, and long-employed, tenured faculty.

As a professional in higher education for more than 25 years, 20 of them devoted to public universities, the author found it most relevant to look at the enrollment management structure at public universities for quite practical reasons. The head of enrollment management needs to constantly review the trends and issues facing all enrollment professionals. Thus, the universities whose enrollment management programs are presented here are public universities identified by leaders in enrollment management research as possible participants in a survey. A conscious effort was made to select a cross-section of universities across the country to investigate possible regional differences. Enrollment management leaders from various public universities agreed to discuss six questions regarding the theory and practice of enrollment management (see Appendix A), to assess their approach to and use of it, and to offer comments and advice to emerging enrollment leaders. The 12 institutions surveyed represent a cross-section of the United States; they are from the East, the Midwest, the Southwest, the South, and the West. They range in size from single campuses with 10,000 students to multiple campuses with 50,000 students or more. The common feature of all these universities is that they have identified themselves or someone has identified them as institutions with an enrollment management structure and/or approach.

The East
University of Maine
The University of Maine includes seven campuses, with 10,000 students at its flagship school at Orono. At this land-grant institution, change has been the only constant. Since 1985, the university system has had two presidents, three interim presidents, six vice presidents, and four different enrollment managers. And it is reorganizing again. Funding for orientation was cut, and the marketing staff was eliminated. Admissions, enrollment management, and records were moved to academic affairs; everything else was placed with student affairs. A new assistant vice president, at the advice of a consultant, will hire a new admissions director and give student affairs a more academic thrust.

An enrollment management system has been in place since 1985. Any positive results of this so-called "charismatic model" have been the result of the personal charisma of the enrollment managers and other administrators' efforts to marshal the forces. With four enrollment managers in 12 years, the outcomes have been uneven. Each new administration had different goals for the institution. The most recent change involved an effort to improve the institution's image and to boost the quality of the student body. One strategy was to sell a two-year campus, which brought the desired increase in quality but also a concomitant decrease in tuition revenue, because fewer students were transferring from the feeder two-year campus. The university's financial situation resulted in the reorganization of student services.

The situation is further complicated by state mandates that the state university reduce its reliance on the state budget for the majority of its funds. Currently, students bear 86 percent of the burden of tuition costs, an amount approaching that of private schools. In addition, raises for faculty must be financed entirely from tuition; hence, the cost of an education at UM has risen significantly.

Representatives from UM view the success of enrollment management as contingent upon the level of support and understanding of everyone involved as to what the institution wants to accomplish. Without everyone on board, progress simply will not happen.*

---

*Joyce Henckler 1997, telephone interview.

University of Connecticut

Enrollment management has been in place at the University of Connecticut since November 1995. The office, described as similar to a division of enrollment management, has a well-articulated mission statement that contains five separate goals:

> *The Office of Enrollment Management at the University of Connecticut . . . [comprises] . . . the Departments of Admissions, Financial Aid, Orientation and Tours, and Scholarship Programs. The mission of the Office is to recruit and select qualified freshmen and transfer students for admission to the University; to oversee their academic progress from entry to graduation; to administer available financial assistance within mandated guidelines; to provide both prospective and new students with a comprehensive introduction to the University; and to identify and reward academically meritorious students available scholarship dollars.**

The Office of Enrollment Management reports to the associate provost for enrollment management, who reports to the vice provost and then to the provost. The associate provost works with an enrollment management advisory committee and a retention advisory committee.

The office has defined evaluation of its efforts as evaluation of "products," including a higher academic profile for the entering class, various brochures on retention and service, a better freshman experience, and more coordination among the various offices. The associate vice provost provides regular reports to the chancellor through the provost's office. Some positive results at UConn are much better coordination among offices in the enrollment management area, synchronized publications and communications, and greater financial support for staffing the areas. The increased visibility of enrollment efforts on campus seems to have resulted in better cooperation among faculty and staff, enabling the enrollment manager to promote the ethical principles and practices espoused by enrollment management professionals and to discuss concerns with the educational community.

---

*Ann Huckenbeck 1997, personal communication.

Commitment and understanding at the very highest level is the only way for enrollment management to succeed. Enrollment managers have a responsibility to educate their superiors about the stumbling blocks to success and keep them apprised of efforts. Without a clear picture of institutional expectations, failure will be the result.

The Midwest
Miami (of Ohio) University

One of 13 state universities in Ohio, Miami is the second oldest university and usually referred to as a "public ivy." The university has three campuses, two regional campuses where technical and parallel baccalaureate courses are taught and the primary campus. The regional campuses are not regarded as feeders to the primary campus but are treated as autonomous units. They have an open admissions policy and handle all their own processing.

The main campus at Oxford has a selective admissions policy and enrolls about 18,000 undergraduate students. What passes for an enrollment management system is a meeting of the deans, provost, and vice presidents, who discuss projected downturns in numbers. The effort is more like a committee than a purposefully created organizational structure. It could be described as an enrollment services model. Many units that affect enrollment cooperate in efforts to bring about the desired enrollment. Evaluation as a management tool relies on simple numbers and course credit hours. An effort is made to identify generally agreed-upon benchmarks and assessment tools with communication through regularly prepared and circulated reports.

An elementary enrollment services model has been in place since 1991. But the general perception on campus is that enrollment management is something one does in response to a crisis. As the vice president for enrollment services indicated, there is no current crisis, so they do not "do" enrollment management. The university has had four presidents in six years, so as long as no crisis exists, the enrollment areas are pretty much left alone. Because the success of enrollment management requires the support of top management, administrators must be convinced that the level of financial and staff support required will definitely benefit the institution.*

---

*James McCoy 1997, personal communication.

The Ohio State University

The Ohio State University is a complex five-campus system spread over most of the central portion of the state. Four regional campuses serve rural populations with an open-admissions policy for first-time freshmen, and the Agricultural Institute serves the whole state by providing one- and two-year technical associate degrees in the agriculture business. Each campus operates independently and is at the same time dependent upon the main campus in Columbus. Some services are centralized; others are provided on the individual campuses. The regional campus enrollment staffs and the one on the main campus are closely affiliated. Therefore, the philosophy and goals of enrollment management are articulated and implemented throughout the system.

The Office of Academic Affairs created the Office of Enrollment Management in September 1995. The individual responsible for all admissions and financial aid at that time was named assistant vice president for enrollment management; the office handled undergraduate, graduate, and transfer admissions, financial aid, university bulletins, and enrollment management decision making, research, and analysis. The assistant vice president works closely with the enrollment steering committee, an advisory committee to the provost chaired by the executive dean of arts and science. The individual also works with a university senate governing committee, the Council on Enrollment and Student Progress.

The office has established a specific mission statement and an extensive list of goals. Ohio State has imported Dolence's definition of strategic enrollment management. It is seen as a comprehensive and universitywide process designed to help Ohio State achieve and maintain the optimum recruitment, retention, and graduation rates for all students (undergraduate, graduate, and professional on all campuses). Enrollment management depends on strategic goal setting and strategic planning, as well as communication of the messages used to attract students, and product decisions and performance. The mission is widely circulated and articulated to all levels of the university.[*]

Borrowing from the four models described by Hossler, the Ohio State model appears to be a mixture of the matrix, divi-

---

[*]James Mager 1997, personal communication.

---

sion, and coordinator models. The sheer size of the university (56,000 students at all campuses, with 48,000 in Columbus) seems to indicate that one single model would not be sufficient. The assistant vice president sits on the Provost's Council (academic affairs) and has access to student affairs, the registrar, business affairs, and all the college deans. Goals and results are communicated through reports to the Council on Enrollment and Student Progress (faculty), the Enrollment Management Steering Committee (all departments and divisions), the Council of Deans (academic administration), and the President's Council. The goals of enrollment management set for the university have made significant progress in the quality and diversity of incoming freshmen. The retention rate has also increased after a four-year decline before formation of the Office of Enrollment Management.

Goals address such areas as the total number of students, retention rates, the academic quality of students, and the geographic and ethnic diversity of students. Success is measured against how closely results match the clear and specific goals established. Enrollment management is also evaluated on how frequently decisions about the allocation of resources are based on the strategy and facts presented to upper administration. The implementation of actions based on facts and research is viewed as the key factor in institutional success.

The assistant vice president counsels that newcomers to enrollment management would be wise to first make sure they have the philosophical support of the upper-level administrators who are willing to collaborate on enrollment efforts at the institution. Fact-based and realistic goals should be established, and financial support must be provided to enable goal-focused research and implementation of the resulting plans. In addition, the head of the institution's enrollment management efforts needs quantitative skills, people skills, and motivation to stay in touch with the art and science of enrollment management as it evolves.

Kent State University
Kent State University is one of 13 state universities in Ohio. The Kent system enrolls 20,000 students on its Kent campus and approximately 10,000 more on its regional campuses located across the northeast and east central portions of the state. The regional campuses are autonomous units, but a

collaborative relationship exists among individual campuses. At the Kent campus, the Division of Enrollment Management is headed by a vice president and dean for enrollment management and student affairs. Two associate vice presidents, one for enrollment services and one for student support services, oversee the majority of the areas within enrollment management. The division has articulated a very specific mission.

> *The mission of the Division of Enrollment Management and Student Affairs is to provide leadership to institutional efforts focused on the co-curricular learning opportunities, services, and programs for students [that] complement and support the mission of the University and thereby assist in maximizing [students'] academic and career success, personal development, health and wellness, institutional vitality, enrollment, and retention.**

In addition to the mission statement, another specific statement deals with "core characteristics." This document directs the actions and activities of the division, and designates specific areas with which individuals in the division interact for implementation of the mission. The characteristics include five specific statements with key phrases such as "promote student learning," "effective recruitment and retention programs," "professionals whose expertise focuses on students," "continual assessment of programs and services," "a supportive environment," "leadership that is student centered and promotes student success," "collaborative processes," and "respecting diversity." The characteristics in this statement appear to incorporate all the key aspects of enrollment management as carried out by the division, which include admissions, career services, the registrar, student financial aid, student research and analysis, adult services, campus life, student disability services, intramural and campus recreation, judicial affairs, residence services, health services, cultural diversity, and three other general areas that deal with personnel, evaluation, and mediation.

This particular structure has been in place since September 1996, and good progress has been made in building a team and starting a good program. It is too soon to be able to eval-

---

*Chuck Rickard 1997, personal communication.

uate the system, but the ultimate evaluation will be the changes in enrollments. Parts of an enrollment management system were in place for a number of years, but then many complicating factors changed the environment of the campus. The institution was plagued with two major problems, image and the cost of tuition (it was recently ranked fourth in cost among state public institutions in Ohio).

The president has been very supportive of the reorganization, and believes that enrollment is everyone's job and responsibility. The sense on campus is that many people are working hard to accomplish goals to increase and manage enrollments on the main campus, for example, the number of new students, the number of returning students, and the graduation rate. There is no sense of progress on retention because of the need for faculty to be involved in that process. Since the current president has been on board, however, faculty seem to be more aware of the need to retain students and to provide links among departments, students, and faculty. A unionized faculty makes the issue more challenging, but the enrollment staff is hopeful that efforts will be successful.

The enrollment division works with a steering committee that deals with enrollment planning, student recruitment, retention, marketing, and size, quality, and diversity of the student body. This committee is advisory to the president and makes recommendations on budgeted enrollment. The model is viewed as dynamic, a work in progress.

Advice offered to newcomers is simple: Understand who the key players are, assign good people to committees, take bold stances on securing allocations, and be committed to the future of the institution.

The Southwest
Arizona State University
Arizona State University enrolls more than 42,000 students. It has two branch campuses, one about 12 years old, the other very new. Located outside Phoenix, ASU is one of three major higher education institutions in the state. The enrollment management cluster has been formally in place since 1991. Despite being called a cluster, it is closer to the division model. It is located within student affairs and has within it the offices of undergraduate admissions (including school relations and new student orientation), financial assistance,

student development, residential life, the registrar, and student information systems. The arrangement has evolved partly as a result of long-time staff; for example, the vice president of enrollment management was formerly the director of admissions.*

The mission statement for enrollment management is considered part of the university's mission, with strategic consideration of the goals for overall enrollment. Some of those goals relate to the freshman class, efforts to increase the retention rate, and number of graduates. All members of the enrollment cluster meet monthly as a committee chaired by the vice president and associate vice president. At times, the comptroller joins the meetings for fiscal planning. It is considered an implementing committee. The provost and vice president for student affairs set policy with the committee, which in turn provides information to them. A number of methods are used to disseminate strategy and results; for example, a number of different groups, academic deans, councils, and associate deans communicate strategy to the campus. Statistical reports and other monthly reports are provided to all these groups and individuals.

Enrollment management is not considered a fad. Parts of the current model have been in place since the mid-1970s, and the development of the organization has evolved over a long time. Enrollment professionals feel more pressure than ever to increase academic standards of incoming classes and to change the profile of students. They also want more professional development to have a more diverse set of skills.

University of Arizona
The University of Arizona, located in Tucson near the United States–Mexico border, enrolls about 35,000 students annually and is heavily committed to minorities. The Division of Enrollment Services and Academic Support was created as a result of downsizing during academic year 1992–93. The university adopted the definition of enrollment management espoused by Hossler, Bean, and Associates (1990). An extensive rationale statement discusses this definition as well as activities, goals, and the specific application of two models—the division model for delivery of service to students

---

*Christine Wilkinson 1997, telephone interview.

and the matrix model for policy decisions—for carrying out the functions of enrollment management.

The Division of Enrollment Services and Academic Support adopted a specific mission, dedicating itself to the recruitment and retention of a diverse and talented student body. The mission includes four goals: (1) the provision of institutional leadership in achievement of goals for enrollment; (2) support of the academic mission; (3) formulation and implementation of policies, processes, and services to maximize students' success; and (4) facilitation of decision making and policy formation through accurate and timely data and analysis.* When the division was formed, seven offices were part of the organization: early outreach, admissions and new student enrollment, student financial aid, registrar, university learning center, career services, and student research. Within the recent past, the Office of Student Research was moved out of the configuration and is now incorporated into a decision and planning support office that reports directly to the provost.

The Division of Enrollment Services and Academic Support is within student affairs but reports to the vice president for student affairs and undergraduate education, and indirectly to the provost/senior vice president for academic affairs. The chief officer holds the title assistant vice president for enrollment services and academic support. His function is clearly delineated in the statement of service priorities, and holds a position of centrality to the university's mission. He directly supervises the units in the division and is an institutional leader in issues involving enrollment management and institutional competitiveness, including assisting in setting system and university goals for the recruitment and retention of the optimal mix and profile of undergraduate, graduate, and professional students. The enrollment officer works with a number of policy committees to set goals, and to form and stabilize alliances between academic and community groups.

The overall statement of performance measurement addresses quality and excellence in a general way. But the specifics of measurement are a combination of internal and external indicators, such as achievement of projections (number enrolled), stated goals for public education that can be reported to the board of regents, retention and gradua-

---

*Jerome Lucido 1997, personal communication.

tion rates, time to degree, and the distribution of various populations within the student body.

Some positive benefits of enrollment management are greater operating efficiency in all areas, greater input into institutional policies, and cohesiveness of the units within enrollment services. While it has been good for the university, enrollment management is not regarded as a panacea. It needs to be viable all the time, not just during crises. Good, measurable goals must be established if the model is to be viable. The individuals responsible must be politically savvy.

The South
Georgia State University
The enrollment services office at Georgia State University is headed by the vice president for student life and enrollment services. An assistant vice president for enrollment services/ registrar, the director of admissions, and the director of student financial aid report to the vice president. Key areas for enrollment management include undergraduate enrollment for first-time college freshmen, with consideration given to available classroom space and the availability of required courses for freshmen. The institution and enrollment services have mission statements.

The plan for Georgia State includes enrollment targets for maintaining the university's "rich diversity" as well as specific goals for the international student population. An enrollment management task force headed by the provost includes the vice president for student life, dean of arts and sciences, associate provost, assistant vice president for enrollment services, director of admissions, and a faculty member. This structure and the committee have only recently been enacted. An initial plan for a comprehensive enrollment management structure was compiled in 1988 and scheduled for implementation, but a change in administration caused many priorities to be shifted. The plan was never allocated funds and only recently was implemented. Thus, the task force has yet to define indicators of success or failure, and a system to evaluate enrollment management. It is anticipated that, once the system is established, it will include targets for enrollment based on age, gender, and ethnicity, as well as targets for various programs of study.*

---

*James E. Scott 1997, personal communicaiton.

University of Central Florida

The University of Central Florida, located near Orlando in the heart of the state, enrolls 22,000 undergraduate students and a total population of 27,400. The Division of Enrollment and Academic Services incorporates a wide variety of offices and functions, including the traditional admissions, financial aid, and university registrar, as well as a number of specialized areas. For example, one such area is named "academic development and retention" but incorporates the functions of orientation, retention, athletics, multicultural activities, and academic resources. Additional functional areas under the umbrella of the division include undergraduate academic procedures, special programs, student outreach, minority programming, state grants, centers of excellence, and lead scholars (a special project). Because of the size of the division, staff are also assigned specifically to budgeting and personnel for the division.

The University of Central Florida's Division of Enrollment and Academic Services has a fairly flat line of responsibility and authority. It is headed by a vice provost. The division's mission, vision, and values statement are disseminated throughout the institution. The mission statement identifies the primary purpose of the division as identification, enrollment, retention, and graduation of targeted student segments. The mission also identifies the functions involved, links within the university as a whole, and internal and external constituencies who both affect and are affected by the institution's actions.* The division is also responsible for the university's marketing plan.

The current structure has been evolving since 1993, when the current vice provost joined the university. Key indicators of success have been defined as retention rates, appropriate money management by unit heads, and good services for clients. Evaluation is carried out both informally and formally. Informal evaluation is based on students' complaints or comments, and formal evaluation refers to the specific mission and objectives for each unit in the division and its manager. Three specific groups are considered in evaluations—students, faculty, and the external constituency—and the bottom line is to increase enrollments.

Support must be clearly delineated from the top down. The president or provost must define what enrollment man-

---

*Thomas Huddleston 1997, personal communication.

agement is and who is to do what. The biggest problem is not knowing what is to be accomplished. Two other issues of concern are not specific to enrollment management but affect higher education in general—need-blind admissions and leveraging financial aid.

East Tennessee State University

Enrollment management at ETSU has a broad scope and purpose, as noted in the title of the individual responsible for enrollment management, associate vice president for admissions, retention, and enrollment management. Enrollment management is directly related to the university's retention program. The operational part of the effort is a joint commitment by the offices of admissions, registration, financial aid, bursar, housing, graduate studies, and institutional effectiveness and planning. The message that is broadly communicated on campus is that enrollment management/student retention is the responsibility of the campus as a whole. Enrollment management at ETSU is best defined as planning, designing, organizing, monitoring, and evaluating the system for student matriculation and progression, and it is described as a "consensus model." A well-defined mission statement is embedded in ETSU's Statement of Vision, Mission and Purpose, and Values, a document that addresses the five-year strategic plan with specific objectives for each unit of the university.*

The president, provost, and vice presidents are strongly committed to and support enrollment management at the institution, and leadership clearly communicates that commitment to students' matriculation and success. Enrollment management is listed as second among institutional priorities for budgeting, behind concerns about accreditation. The associate vice president for admissions, retention, and enrollment management reports to the provost and vice president for academic affairs. The provost reports directly to the president. A director of admissions and a director of financial aid report to the associate vice president. A well-established committee structure provides broad input into the planning and decision-making process for enrollment management.

The university president undertook this major effort in 1993. Its primary purpose was to directly involve the major offices associated with enrollment management, five schools

---

*Nancy Dishner 1997, personal communication.

and colleges, departmental chairs, and faculty in enrollment management. The focus on recruitment and retention of undergraduate and graduate students is well under way; it involves individuals at all levels and positions on the campus.

Specific goals for recruitment and retention are defined for the governing board and are reviewed annually. Effort and goals from the previous year are reviewed in a continuing cycle. Key indicators of success include students' ability to receive the services they desire (courses requested, financial assistance, opportunities for scholarships, the availability of programs, advising, retention intervention programs, for example) and progress to graduation. These efforts are reviewed by the governing board, the president's senior staff, the president's council, the academic council, and a variety of other committees and task forces with specific charges. The matriculation rate from freshman to sophomore year has improved modestly, and the continuous improvement initiative to improve academic advisement initiated in 1995 is expected to continue to improve this percentage.

Representatives indicate they have learned that it takes the whole village to successfully implement enrollment management, and that it is necessary to ignore the naysayers to keep on track. Without support from the highest authority, efforts to change the institution's enrollment will not happen. A clear focus on students and on the institution's aims must be maintained at all times.

University of Memphis

Since 1994, the University of Memphis has been undergoing change, starting with a name change, the reorganization of various offices to form the Division of Enrollment Management, and employment of an individual who views his job as a bridge between student affairs and academic affairs. The dual title vice president for student affairs and vice provost for enrollment services helps bring about a culture that includes all aspects of the university in the recruitment and retention of students. The vice president for student affairs reports to the president and sits on the President's Council. As the vice provost for enrollment services, the individual reports to the provost and sits on the Provost's Council. The overall mission of enrollment services has been to look comprehensively at the recruitment of students, determine the quality of students desired, and consider the quality of customer service.

One of the key institutions embroiled in discussions of enrollment management during the 1980s was Cal State at Los Angeles.

A 35-person enrollment management council, which meets monthly, is headed by the provost and vice provost. It is considered a policy-making group. Every area of the university is represented: academic affairs, academic deans, department chairs, and all administrative units that affect the recruitment of students. An executive committee of the council meets more frequently to identify resources for recruitment and retention and to implement policy recommendations. A retention committee incorporates student affairs, publications, the African-American student group, and off-campus offerings to work with the enrollment management council and to act as liaison with offices affecting enrollment.

The effort took three years to get started. Goals and issues include better retention rates, the quality of services to continuing students, courses with especially high failure rates, and liaison or coordination with the academic community. After three years, some faculty still resisted getting involved. Incompatible data systems slowed efforts to collect and analyze the data necessary to accurately project and evaluate efforts. Nevertheless, the vice provost indicates that although progress has been slower than desired, strides have been made in getting more parts of the university community to accept responsibility for enrollment issues.*

To the present time, the university continues to follow the Shirley strategic planning model, named after Dr. Robert Shirley.

The West
California State University at Los Angeles
One of the key institutions embroiled in discussions of enrollment management during the 1980s was Cal State at Los Angeles. To the present time, the university continues to follow the Shirley strategic planning model, named after Dr. Robert Shirley, president of the University of Southern Colorado. But it is not the enrollment management model as originally designed. No one was ever appointed to head the system that was designed, because sufficient funds were not allocated to permit the model to be implemented. The provost who has headed the effort since 1995 articulates a definition of enrollment management as a process by which the institution moves toward improved graduation rates and increases the proportion of students who enter prepared to complete baccalaureate education. It is an effort to control enrollments so as to maximize resources and demonstrate success in the graduation rate.

---

*Donald Carson 1997, personal communication.

The model is described as a matrix. Faculty serve on all committees, including the retention committee, which includes a representative from each school, the dean of undergraduate studies (who chairs the committee), students, representatives from the student union, learning services, the educational opportunities program, financial affairs, and a faculty member from the basic academic skills area. The vice president for student affairs chairs the recruitment task force, which includes the director of admissions and outreach, the dean of graduate studies, two school deans, representatives from the offices of public affairs, student affairs, financial aid, and alumni, and two additional appointed faculty members. The biggest problem is convincing the campus community of the effort's worth, as, across the institution, few take enrollment management seriously. Nevertheless, a written enrollment management plan essentially plans enrollment targets for the short term. Monitoring is limited. A plan is currently in place to institute a strategic planning council that reports to the president. Results of implemented policies are disseminated across the campus through fact sheets.

The recruitment task force, which reports to the president, considers projections, targets, demographic data, and state and board decrees for their impact on enrollment. A retention task force is charged with meeting the targets for enrollment for new admits. Goals for new admits were met in July 1996, with the hope for better results in 1997.* Revising goals to look at particular majors was under consideration for 1998. The retention-to-graduation task force concentrates on improving retention in the first two years of school. A five-year strategic plan has been implemented to improve retention from the first to the second year to 90 percent, with a 50 percent graduation rate within six years.

The institution uses key performance indicators to measure success and to provide a basis for setting priorities for funding. The most important indicator is the number of admissions in the "special admit" category, a specific problem population that the board has decreed be reduced. These students are admitted by special action, despite questionable or very low academic results. The average rate of persistence for this population is very low, the graduation rate less than 18 percent. This type of special action presents a seri-

*Margaret Hartman 1997, personal communication.

ous concern, as students should have a good probability of graduating if they are admitted. Therefore, discussion continues to center on limiting enrollment to students who have the highest chance for success in completing college.

Summary of Current Practices in Public Universities

A total of 12 public universities participated in the survey and interviews, which investigated 10 basic areas: definitions and key elements of enrollment management, mission statements, structure, evaluation, key indicators of success, communication of results, duration and durability, successes and adjustments, ethical concerns, and advice to the novice.

Definitions and key elements of enrollment management

All 12 institutions surveyed included admission as a part of the definition of enrollment management, 10 included financial aid, and nine included records, registration, or the registrar's office. One-half the institutions reported research and analysis as part of the formal configuration or a related service for the area of enrollment management. Only two specifically mentioned a retention office, although all mentioned a goal of increased retention or reduced attrition of students.

Mission statements

A majority of the institutions interviewed had a specific mission for enrollment services or enrollment management. That mission was sometimes a detailed statement of organization, goals and objectives, and methods of evaluation. At other times, the mission was simply a description of the offices or functions involved and general statements relating to goals for enrollment.

Structure

More than half the institutions described the structure for enrollment management as a division. (Hossler's delineation [1986] describes the division as the most complex model and the one with the greatest probability of success.) Although the individuals listed as chief enrollment officer held a variety of titles, efforts were more successful at institutions where that position reports to a provost or vice provost. Almost as many positions reported to both academic affairs and student affairs as to academic affairs alone. Despite student affairs's having given birth to enrollment management through admissions offices in years past, this reporting structure was listed last in terms of current practice among the large public universities surveyed.

Evaluation

The institutions surveyed carried out evaluation both informally and formally. In some institutions, funding for the unit was tied to meeting established goals. Most places sought students' input for evaluation, either through a system to garner complaints or surveys of students' satisfaction, in considering particular campus-related goals. The establishment of specific targets for various student groups provided benchmarks for evaluation of enrollment efforts.

Key indicators of success

Key indicators of successful enrollment management related to the goals established. Every institution listed the bottom line for enrollment—enrollment by geographic area, program, academic quality (including standardized test scores and cumulative GPAs), and diversity. A majority of the institutions surveyed also mentioned graduation rate and time to degree as goals to be achieved. Beyond these three indicators, they agreed very little. Institutions where principles of quality management prevailed listed quality service, fiscal management of units, and increased cooperation among units as key factors of success.

Communication of results

Every institution used a variety of committees, councils, or task forces (variously called retention task forces, recruitment committees, resource planning committees, and implementation committees) to implement the goals and objectives of enrollment management and to communicate to the campus and the community. The chief enrollment management officer was involved in some way with most of these groups. Committees and task forces were organized to incorporate the units in enrollment management and academic disciplines, and the administrative areas related to fiscal management.

Duration and durability

Not all the universities surveyed cited enrollment management as a specific organizational structure. In at least three instances, a specific plan had been introduced a decade earlier, but internal and external institutional factors caused the plan to be shelved. Parts of those plans have been reintroduced recently at two of the universities. Of the remaining institutions, an identifiable structure had been in place for one to six years at the time of the survey.

Successes and adjustments

A majority of the individuals representing the public universities identified "success" as attaining specific goals for enrollment and diversity, and increased communication and cooperation on campus. Retention was the hardest goal to measure accurately, although some could point to better graduation rates and changes in the curriculum that allow students to complete degrees in four years if they are enrolled full time.

Ethical concerns

The question of ethics drew a wide range of responses, from no concerns to serious concerns about such issues as need-blind admissions, policies for awarding financial aid, and conflict between professional organizations and the university. One individual's response to the question of ethics— you do the right thing, you do it to the best of your ability, and you treat other people as you would want to be treated—was the prevailing attitude. Most enrollment officers believe that fairness, disclosure, consideration, and honesty from members of the institution toward all constituencies will lead to successfully attaining goals.

Advice to the novice

Every institutional representative pointed out the same pitfalls—lack of fiscal resources and personnel and lack of clarity for attempted goals. These individuals clearly implied that institutions must stay focused on students. It is only by doing what is in the best interests of students that any institution can hope to succeed. And a focus on students' success can happen only if the institution's leadership is committed to students. Moreover, that commitment must be articulated vertically as well as horizontally. Although enrollment management will always be a struggle, efforts will succeed if the president is committed to the program and endorses a student-centered focus for the institution.

CONCLUSIONS

It is clear that enrollment management professionals from around the country find it relatively easy to discuss the components of enrollment management models and the techniques used to implement or maintain the goals of those models. The hardest part is probably differentiating the practices and explaining why the theory works at one institution and fails at another. Many current practitioners have a background in recruitment, admissions, or financial aid; hence, the emphasis, perhaps because of the history of a model, remains mostly within the realm of student services.

Structure and Mission

Most practitioners at large public universities can articulate well the goals for entering students and the bottom line for enrollments and for tuition income. Many individuals can also define enrollment management in terms that are almost verbatim from the primary theorists. Most can provide a well-articulated response to the expected outcomes of following the model. But rather than having a specific definition for enrollment management, most institutional representatives define the organizational structure of the office, division, committee, or task force by the areas included in the structure and the mission of the particular configuration. For example, the mission of the Office of Enrollment Management at the University of Connecticut is to recruit and select qualified freshman and transfer students for admission; to oversee their academic progress; to provide financial assistance within mandated guidelines; to provide prospective and new students with a comprehensive introduction to the university; and to identify and reward academically meritorious students with available scholarships.*

At East Tennessee State University, enrollment management is described in action terms, such as planning, designing, organizing, monitoring, and evaluating the system for the matriculation and progression of students. At California State–Los Angeles, enrollment management is referred to as a process by which the institution moves toward an improved graduation rate as well as increases the proportion of entering students prepared to do baccalaureate-level work. At Georgia State, enrollment management is defined as more of a goal, "comprising undergraduate enrollment for

---

*Ann Huckenbeck 1997, personal communication.

first-time . . . college freshmen, with consideration given to classroom space available and with regard to the availability of required courses for freshmen."*

Three General Goals of Enrollment Management

When all the comments are taken together, enrollment management appears to have three general goals: to increase enrollment, to create a student body that meets the goals and expectations of institutional policy makers, and to achieve better institutional graduation rates.

Most, if not all, the practitioners can point to specific examples of how the first two goals have been or are being met. Many institutions have witnessed definite positive changes with regard to planned enrollment goals. A specific goal at Ohio State, for example, was to increase the academic profile within five years, using high school rank and ACT composite scores as two measures. In fact, the number of honor students and presidential scholarship–caliber enrollees increased, and the ACT composite moved up nearly two points in three years. At Arizona State, the retention rate and diversity and quality indicators showed steady improvement.

In some places, increases can be partially attributed to changes in state requirements. In Georgia, for example, resident students who had earned a B average upon graduation from high school and attend one of the state universities receive a state scholarship covering a large portion of their tuition. At Georgia State, 70 to 75 percent of a recent class of 2,000 freshmen was eligible for a Hope Scholarship. In addition, state regents forced the growth of all institutions by establishing enrollment goals for all 34 state schools. The growth is projected over five to six years, within a 2 percent range. Deviations over or under the required range impact funding. Georgia State is expected to grow from 24,000 to 26,000 by the turn of the century.

The third goal, better graduation rates, seems harder to pinpoint as a direct outcome of enrollment management. Retention programs have gained extensive recognition as the public clamors for greater institutional accountability and demonstrations of quality goods received for money invested. Retention has been described as a campus-wide effort to improve students' persistence to graduation, which

---

*James E. Scott 1997, personal communication.

affects both individuals and society. The benefits of persistence appear to last across a lifetime, and from a broad viewpoint, retention of students to graduation is in the best interests of our society. Large numbers of students leaving college before completing a degree gives the impression that institutions are failing their customers.

The Value and Credibility of Higher Education

In the strictest business sense, customers (students, their families, and the general public) demand more value for their money—and perhaps with good reason. Some professionals in the field have called for the restoration of credibility to higher education (Mahoney 1996), starting with admissions professionals, who have sometimes been seen as hucksters driven by the demographic realities of the 1980s and early 1990s. During that time, the public's perception of higher education was altered by many of the practices that overshadowed the counseling aspect of admissions with marketing and leveraging enrollments. Other parts of institutions were similarly involved in actions that attracted the attention of state and national legislators, however. Urged on by hungry media and a distraught public, higher education was taken to task, put under a magnifying glass, and found to be wanting. Institutional and industry policies that forced families to pit one school against another to gain the best financial package gave the impression of a feeding frenzy.

One way to restore credibility with some constituencies is to focus on outcomes-based research.

A multitude of vendors also took advantage of the situation by creating new technologies and services that were supposed to help students. Some were valuable, but many others just added to the impression that those involved in higher education were looking out for themselves and not for students or their families—for example, financial assistance services that played upon families' naivete and charged a fee for information that is available free of charge in high school guidance offices, from college financial aid officers, or in public libraries.

One way to restore credibility with some constituencies is to focus on outcomes-based research, that is, show that we do what we say we do in our promotional materials. Claims of employment for graduates, acceptances to graduate schools, graduates' ability to pay off loans, and reasonable time to complete a degree all need to be substantiated to demonstrate to the public and to our own students and their families that their investment is worth the time and the money.

An Evaluation of Quality

Higher education institutions have been reluctant to demonstrate their value through measurements the public can understand. Many activities related to admissions, however, are convenient yardsticks to measure success and are easy to understand. For example, goals for admission and enrollment, such as targets for enrollment and entering students' class rank, GPA, and SAT/ACT scores, are broadly available and easily quantified. Although most of these quantifications do not really relate to the outcomes of higher education, the public would like to see measures of outcome they can understand. Quality improvement, total quality management, national standards, and performance evaluation have not traditionally been part of university management.

> *For an enterprise purportedly driven by rationality and empiricism, the academy may be surprisingly vulnerable to charges that it often fails to follow its own credo, that its programs, policies, and procedures are shaped as much by unchallenged assumptions and hopeful visions as by data* (McGowan 1996, p. 4).

Universities routinely produce significant research and new technology that address business and industry's needs but rarely apply these principles to themselves. Evaluation must address the concerns of all constituencies, on and off campus. A comprehensive scheme would address both people and programs. The difficulty of evaluating the effect of specific college or university activities on people does not relieve the higher education industry of the responsibility of trying to measure impact. In an age of accountability, the value of higher education must be demonstrated, not assumed.

Enrollment management activities lend themselves to measuring such areas as quality service, student, staff, and faculty attitude, and change in economic status after completion of college. With regard to quality service, higher education simply cannot afford to ignore the way students are treated on campus. Students constantly judge whether or not their institution really cares about them. Daily contacts are the real test of how well an institution fulfills its marketing promises. Institutions can substantially strengthen their image and student retention rates with efforts to develop positive and effective customer relations through better service.

Only in the recent past have institutions of higher education taken active steps to improve the quality of services on their campuses. These efforts have paid off, with increased staff productivity, decreased costs, and a more enterprising attitude on the part of faculty and administrators. For example, one president decided to recognize the role secretaries play by inviting them to appreciation breakfasts. He explained that these key staff members set the tone for a campus when they talk to students and others in person or over the telephone. Such recognition of the importance of their contributions, along with quality training, sends messages to staff of respect and appreciation. In turn, the effort improves staff members' morale and ultimately improves services to students and other staff and faculty—creating a win/win situation.

Quality service on campus has been shown to be a key element in attracting and retaining students. The structure of enrollment management maintains the efficiency necessary for complex organizations to operate but enough flexibility to be user friendly and student centered. These arrangements help to counter negative images that hurt enrollment, especially if the institution has been considered too impersonal. The goal of all enrollment management systems should be to ensure that the institution is responsive to students' needs and to create a student-centered campus.

Virtually every conversation on enrollment management discusses the improvement of teamwork among departments on campus and better service to students. Both messages take their direction from the quality movement sweeping higher education from the mailroom to the classroom. Teamwork and improved service to students are easiest to assess in those service areas outside the academic sanctum of professors' classes. The paper flow and computerized systems of financial aid processes, billing and posting payments, scheduling classes, posting grades, and generating grade reports and transcripts can be regulated and evaluated with many principles of quality control. Because all these enrollment service areas involve and serve students, these offices can evaluate and modify distinct operations that appear to lead to satisfied customers.

The Role of Faculty

The improvement of quality in the face of constraints on revenue must involve faculty, coordination of top-down leadership with bottom-up management, and simplification of the organization. The actual process of education, that endeavor that takes place between teacher and student, is not so easily dissected. The student-consumer's satisfaction is sometimes arbitrarily attributed to grades, the professor's teaching style, the student's interest in the subject matter and motivation to learn, and other intangible characteristics. The academic classroom is the single most important area of the institution over which an enrollment management plan holds no sway except for the loyalty, desire, and belief of faculty that they hold the key to the retention and graduation of students. Faculty are therefore integral to a successful enrollment management model.

Although the quality of the academic enterprise is in the hands of faculty, some issues regarding the term "quality" inhibit acceptance of the activities useful in enhancing students' educational experience. For example, faculty might be reluctant to consider students as partners in the learning process. Faculty might find it easier to relate to students as beneficiaries of the educational process who can articulate many of their own needs and interact intelligently with them.

In a number of ways, faculty are eager to endorse concepts of quality service. Most faculty members take great pride in providing excellence in the classroom. Thus, they may already use some principles of quality. For example, most faculty request input from students in evaluating their teaching, and information gathered frequently assists faculty to critique their own attitudes and interactions with students (in addition to fulfilling the required administrative purposes). Faculty and academic departments can operate cooperatively with enrollment management offices to evaluate students' perceptions and attitudes about all parts of the educational experience. The use of various student and faculty surveys enables all constituents on campus to have a say in what transpires and to receive feedback on their own efforts.

Quality service is an outgrowth of the desire of college and university administrators and faculty to eliminate factors from campus that interfere with a positive learning environment; that is, they want to create an environment conducive to the delivery of a quality education. One Noel-Levitz survey of students listed a caring attitude of faculty and staff as number one among the top 10 reasons students remain in college (Richter *n.d.,* p. 1). Therefore, every person who comes in contact with students needs to pay attention to the quality of every interaction between a student and institutional representatives. This attention pays off in better retention rates and more satisfied students, which translates into supportive alumni. The activities also provide data that the general public can easily understand, allowing them to understand the goals of higher education more readily.

Advice to the Novice

When advice is given to new practitioners, the primary message is clear: Get a commitment from top administrators and plenty of resources for major institutional change, which appears to translate into money. The biggest challenge in enrollment management is to involve and garner the support of all constituencies. It costs money, so financial support must be in place or the effort will fail to get off the ground. Every one of the practitioners surveyed mentioned a need for commitment from the highest authority in the institution and, second, the commitment of significant funds and personnel to permit the operation of a comprehensive enrollment management system. Most also acknowledged that such a system gears up during crisis and is more or less ignored during times of plenty.

Many practitioners also acknowledged that the success of the enrollment plan has much to do with the influence and charisma of the enrollment management leader. Someone who exudes the personal magnetism that attracts an almost Svengali-like following of those involved in enrollment management seems to generate the most successful program and the most support of upper management. Frequently, this individual is an upper manager with especially powerful influence over colleagues and peers—which is not to imply that average, motivated, hard-working managers do not lead successful enrollment programs. The vast majority of individuals in this field are exactly that. Frequently, however, when the leader moves on to another institution or is kicked upstairs, the movement loses its momentum and is either simply maintained or even falters and dies, only to be reinvented by another new administrator in a few years, usually during a crisis.

Enrollment managers are faced with dilemmas that strike at the heart of their profession with competing demands from the administration and their professional organizations.

Ethical Dilemmas

Enrollment managers are faced with dilemmas that strike at the heart of their profession with competing demands from the administration and their professional organizations. The gravest concern expressed by practitioners deals with ethical conflicts between their institution and principles of practice as expressed by such organizations as the National Association of College Admission Counselors, the American Association of Collegiate Registrars and Admissions Officers, and the National Association of Student Financial Aid Administrators. Such conflicts deal with the informal agreement to give students to May 1 to decide which school to attend, students already committed to other institutions, and slanted statements that criticize or impugn others. Some managers expressed concern that the demands for loyalty to the institution at all costs were reminiscent of bygone corporate families: the institution right or wrong!

Discounting tuition and leveraging financial aid are practices borrowed from business management books. Tuition discounting is a significant selling point for some students at some institutions, particularly in the private sector. But it may be a practice that benefits only a few, because the cost of education at a private school is not partially underwritten by the state. Instead, all the other students at a private institution may end up paying for the discounts provided for a few. Discounting has not emerged as much of an issue in the public sector yet, because public institutions do not have a great deal of flexibility to significantly modify a student's portion of the cost of education. Scholarship aid has increased somewhat, but a majority of scholarship money is from private sources and may be highly restrictive. At state universities seeking to increase certain target populations from outside the state, for example, a privately funded scholarship may offset a portion of the surcharge for nonresidents as an inducement for a nonresident to enroll. Whether or not such offsetting or discounting serves the student well is cause for concern if the decision to attend an institution is based primarily on the financial aid package offered.

Leveraging financial aid, another practice currently in vogue at both private and public institutions, allows the use of limited financial aid dollars for those who are neediest and most qualified who would probably not attend without significant financial assistance. Those who are already committed to attend or who appear to have the most financial resources are not included in the leveraging equation. The perceived benefit sounds reasonable—use limited funds to entice and enroll the type of student wanted who would otherwise not attend and increase the percentage of students who pay their own way and would come regardless of any aid provided—but is this practice fair or ethical? Some professionals believe it is unethical only if no disclosure of the fact occurs, yet it is a concern for a significant portion of enrollment management practitioners.

In an era of increased accountability, legislatively imposed performance standards that seem to bear little resemblance to the highest goals of education, and reduced public funding for both students and institutions, higher education administrators are challenged to balance the traditional goals of a university degree with the demands and realities of society. Enrollment management can provide the tools and direction to craft at least part of the response to this challenge.

SUMMARY AND RECOMMENDATIONS

Two questions recurred during researching, discussing, and writing this volume: (1) What have we learned in more than two decades of enrollment management? and (2) Where are we going? If we look simply at the strides in technology, attention to quality teaching and service, and efforts at marketing and retention, an easy conclusion would be that we have learned much.

We have advanced far beyond higher education for only the privileged few who could afford it. Individuals in the business of recruiting and admitting students, and managing students' records have formed a highly respected profession where knowledge of marketing, financial management, statistics, and projective techniques is more important than shuffling papers or traveling to the most distant high school. In public higher education, admissions professionals have gone from gatekeepers to marketers, motivators, fortune tellers, and public relations specialists. They have gone from making personal presentations to a select few in schools, offices, or homes to preparing market analyses of territories and trend analyses of projected high school graduation classes. They have become not only authorities on institutional admission and financial aid policies, but also partners in enrollment decisions affecting the whole institution as well as individual students. Those responsible for enrollment are no longer located only in admissions and registration. Now they are all over the campus, planning with faculty how best to assist students with learning problems, or discussing cafeteria food, physical facilities, or other services that seem to be causing dissatisfaction among students. Many enrollment management professionals are institutional researchers or have access to an institutional research department to track students throughout their educational careers and provide crucial data to the president's cabinet for important decisions. Enrollment management professionals work harder at knowing students all the way through the educational process. They endeavor to provide students with the best possible environment in which to finish their education.

Yet the percentage of students who finish their college education is dropping, to under 50 percent in a recent report (Ohio Board 1996). Despite all we have learned and all we have done, a serious problem persists: Some individuals who are qualified and choose college with high hopes are unable to achieve their dreams. Practices such as discounting tuition and leveraging financial aid are troublesome from the perspective of student services, although they are sound business practices in noneducational organizations. These and other business-borrowed practices will be greatly questioned as we move into the next century.

A successful enrollment management program fundamentally changes the way institutions perceive their clientele, confront challenges, exploit opportunities, and manage resources. An unsuccessful program is based on flawed planning, insufficient participation and personnel, and inadequate fiscal resources. When it is successful, enrollment management modifies the institutional decision-making process and provides for greater involvement of all constituencies on campus.

In the future, it will be even more critical that enrollment managers broaden their own knowledge base and involvement with every facet of the institution. We have become very good at marketing our institutions and at producing well-designed and attractive publications based on market surveys and on students' expectations and attitudes. We have developed complex data systems that are capable of tracking students individually and as members of a group. We use surveys of students to point out trouble spots on campus and work toward eliminating the problems identified.

We spend a great deal of time and effort on the process of attracting students, and some time on creating a pleasing environment for their education. We do not, however, spend much time on evaluating the educational process or outcomes. Retention and outcomes-based research on our graduates would provide extremely valuable information and enable our institutions to strengthen programs of study and revise them as necessary. This type of research needs to be initiated in cooperation with faculty members. Such collaboration would complete the circle of an institution-wide effort.

Moreover, we cannot move into the next century without recognizing the huge changes that technology has brought to higher education. The whole definition of a college or university is constantly being refined as entire curricula are offered over the Internet or through distance learning and other interactive technologies. The definition of a student is also changing. Just a few short years ago, we began discussing the "nontraditional" student and learned to adjust to the needs of a slightly older student population; now we discuss students whom we may never see on campus. How do we meet their needs, and how do we ensure a quality education for them? What is their relationship to the institution from which they earn credit, even degrees? How do we "manage" enrollment when our student population is seated at computer terminals all around the country? How do we determine or maintain institutional quality? What role does financial aid play in an institution that is on-line? Where does enrollment management fit in this new age?

The on-line, "virtual" college or university is not a futuristic vision; it already exists for a growing number of individuals. These students resist the more traditional university setting and challenge our views about classrooms, teaching methods, services, evaluation, and outcomes. Thus, although enrollment management can take us into the next century using good, sound educational and business practices to ensure the efficient and effective operation of our universities as they currently exist, it will have to adapt to the changing environment to meet the challenges we face with new educational models. Enrollment management must continue to be as dynamic in the 21st century as it has been for the last 25-plus years of the 20th century, evolving and changing to meet tomorrow's needs.

APPENDIX A: Enrollment Management Survey and Interview Guide

1. Define enrollment management for your own institution, including key areas or elements. Do you have a mission statement? What is it?

2. What is the structure used to implement and support enrollment management? Who heads the effort? Who reports to whom? Do you have an organizational chart or plan showing the relationships? Hossler identified four models of enrollment management: committee, coordinator, matrix, division. Would you identify your structure as similar to one of them? Which one?

3. How do you evaluate enrollment management efforts at your institution? What appear to be key indicators of success or failure? How do you communicate results and to whom?

4. How long has your structure been in place? Any success stories to share? What have you (and your institution) learned, and how have you adjusted? Where are you going from here?

5. What ethical concerns or considerations do you have with regard to enrollment management?

6. What advice would you give to a colleague whose institution is considering a change to enrollment management? What advice would you give to someone who is struggling with the structure?

REFERENCES

The Educational Resources Information Center (ERIC) Clearinghouse on Higher Education abstracts and indexes the current literature on higher education for inclusion in ERIC's database and announcement in ERIC's monthly bibliographic journal, *Resources in Education* (RIE). Most of these publications are available through the ERIC Document Reproduction Service (EDRS). For publications cited in this bibliography that are available from EDRS, ordering number and price code are included. Readers who wish to order a publication should write to the ERIC Document Reproduction Service, 7420 Fullerton Road, Suite 110, Springfield, Virginia 22153-2852. (Phone orders with VISA or MasterCard are taken at (800) 443-ERIC or (703) 440-1400.) When ordering, please specify the document (ED) number. Documents are available as noted in microfiche (MF) and paper copy (PC). If you have the price code ready when you call, EDRS can quote an exact price. The last page of the latest issue of *Resources in Education* also has the current cost, listed by code.

Albright, J. Winter 1986. "Enrollment Management: Successor to Marketing or Its Synonym?" *College and University* 61: 114–16.

American Council on Education. 29 January 1990. "Facts in Brief." *Higher Education and National Affairs.* Washington, D.C.: Author.

Backer, R. June/July 1987. "Enrollment Management: A Practitioner's Perspective. Kent State University: A Case Study." Paper presented at a meeting of the College Board, New Orleans, Louisiana, and Evanston, Illinois.

Baldridge, J.V., F.R. Kemerer, and K. Green, eds. 1982. *Enrollments in the 80s: Factors, Actors, and Impacts.* Washington, D.C.: American Association for Higher Education.

Baum, S. Fall 1994. "Will Higher Education Affordability Be the Health Care Issue of the 21st Century?" *College Board Review* 173: 8–13+.

Bean, J.P. 1990. "Why Students Leave: Insights from Research." In *The Strategic Management of College Enrollments,* edited by D. Hossler, J.P. Bean, and Associates. San Francisco: Jossey-Bass.

Beeler, Karl J., and Pamela J. Moehl. Summer 1996. "Continuous Improvement: A Way of Integrating Student Enrollment, Advising, and Retention Systems in a Metropolitan University." *Metropolitan Universities: An International Forum* 6(4): 17–33.

Benson, Gordon L. 1993. "The Chair's Role in College Enrollment Management: Matriculation of Students." Paper presented at the Second International Conference for Community College Chairs,

Deans, and Other Instructional Leaders, February, Phoenix, Arizona. ED 354 036. 85 pp. MF-01; PC-04.

Bents, Mary, and Catherine Haugen. Spring 1992. "An Enrollment Management Model for Increasing Diversity." *College and University* 67(3): 195–201.

Boger, Ruth E. Winter 1994. "Involving Graduate Assistants in Student Retention Efforts." *College and University* 69(2): 100–103.

Bok, D. 1982. *Beyond the Ivory Tower.* Cambridge, Mass.: Harvard Univ. Press.

Boughan, Karl. 1995. "Enrollment Management Targeting by PG-TRAK90: Cluster Analyzing Cohort 1990 Four-Year Outcomes Groups." Market Analysis MA95-5. Largo, Md.: Prince Georges Community College. ED 380 164. 12 pp. MF-01; PC-01.

Bowen, H.R. 1977. *Investment in Learning: The Individual and Social Value of American Higher Education.* San Francisco: Jossey-Bass.

Breneman, D.W. March 1983a. "The Coming Enrollment Crisis." *Change* 15(2): 14–19.

———. 1983b. "The Coming Enrollment Crisis: What Every Trustee Must Know." Washington, D.C.: Association of Governing Boards of Universities and Colleges. ED 226 649. 40 pp. MF-01; PC not available EDRS.

———. 7 March 1997. "The Privatization of Public Universities: A Mistake or a Model for the Future?" *Chronicle of Higher Education* 42(26): B4–B5.

Bryant, Peter, and Kevin Crockett. Fall 1993. "The Admissions Office Goes Scientific." *Planning for Higher Education* 22(1): 1–8.

Caberera, A., et al. 1993. "College Persistence: Structural Equations Modeling Test of an Integrated Model of Student Retention." *Journal of Higher Education* 64(2): 123–29.

"Can College Tuition Reductions Increase Enrollment and Quality?" October 1997. *Enrollment Management Report* 1(7): 1+.

Chaffee, E.E., and L.A. Sherr. 1992. *Quality: Transforming Postsecondary Education.* ASHE-ERIC Higher Education Report No. 3. Washington, D.C.: George Washington Univ., Graduate School of Education and Human Development. ED 351 922. 145 pp. MF-01; PC-06.

Chait, R.P. September/October 1987. "Third and Long for Enrollment Managers." *Change* 19(5): 43–45.

Claffey, M.A., and D. Hossler. March 1986. "An Integrated Enrollment Management System." In *Managing College Enrollments,* edited by D. Hossler. New Directions for Higher Education No. 53. San Francisco: Jossey-Bass.

Clagett, Craig A. 1995. "Implementing Successful Enrollment Management: A Conceptual Framework and Two Examples." Paper presented at the Seventh Annual Summer Institute on Institutional Effectiveness and Student Success, June 19, Tacoma, Washington. ED 382 274. 29 pp. MF-01; PC-02.

Clagett, Craig A., and Helen S. Kerr. November 1992. "An Information Infrastructure for Enrollment Management: Tracking and Understanding Your Students." ED 351 075. 14 pp. MF-01; PC-01.

———. Fall 1993. "Tracking and Understanding Your Students." *Planning for Higher Education* 22(1): 9–15.

———. 1994. "Take Charge of Your Enrollment: Improving Enrollment Management through Policy Analysis." Paper presented at the 29th Annual Conference of the Society for College and University Planning, July 25, San Francisco, California. ED 374 875. 18 pp. MF-01; PC-01.

Cohen, A.F., and J.E. King. 1995. "Public Policy Update: Implications for College Admissions." *College Board Review* 176/177: 46–55.

College Board. 1997. "A Report on the College Board Colloquium on the Role of Ethics in Enrollment Management and Financial Aid," January 31–February 1, 1997, Safety Harbor, Florida. New York: Author.

Crane, P. April 1991. "A Tool, Not a Magic Wand—The Limits of Geodemographics." *CASE Currents:* 46–47.

Crockett, D.S. 1993a. "The Enrollment Management Team as Change Agent." Paper presented at the Ohio ACT Assembly, January, Columbus, Ohio. Littleton, Colo.: Williams & Crockett, Noel-Levitz Center for Enrollment Management.

———. 1993b. "Fall 1992 National Enrollment Management Survey Results: Implications for the Enrollment Management Team." Paper presented at the Ohio ACT Assembly, January, Columbus, Ohio. Littleton, Colo.: Williams & Crockett, Noel-Levitz Center for Enrollment Management.

Dehne, George C. May/June 1994. "Reinventing Student Recruitment." *Trusteeship* 2(3): 11–15.

Dixon, R.R., ed. 1995. *Making Enrollment Management Work.* New Directions for Student Services No. 71. San Francisco: Jossey-Bass.

Dolence, M.G. 1988. "Strategic Enrollment Planning and Management." Paper presented at an annual meeting of the Society for College and University Planning, July, Toronto, Ontario.

———. 1989. "Evaluation Criteria for an Enrollment Management Program." Paper presented at a meeting of the Society for College and University Planning, July, Denver, Colorado.

———. 1993. "Strategic Enrollment Management: A Primer for

Campus Administrators." Washington, D.C.: American Association of Collegiate Registrars and Admissions Officers. ED 384 326. 29 pp. MF-01; PC not available EDRS.

———, ed. 1996. *Strategic Enrollment Management: Cases from the Field*. Washington, D.C.: American Association of Collegiate Registrars and Admissions Officers.

Dolence, M.G., D.H. Miyahara, J. Grajeda, and C. Rapp. 1987. "Strategic Enrollment Management and Planning." *Planning for Higher Education* 16(3): 55–74.

Donhardt, G.L. September/October 1995. "Tracking Student Enrollments Using the Markov Chain, Comprehensive Tool for Enrollment Management." *Journal of College Student Development* 36(5): 457–62.

Edmondson, B. March 1997. "Demographics: Keeping Up with Change." *College Board Review* 180: 25–30.

El-Khawas, E. 1994. "Restructuring Initiatives in Public Higher Education: Institutional Response to Financial Constraints." *Research Briefs* 5(8). Washington, D.C.: American Council on Education, Div. of Policy Analysis and Research. ED 377 753. 10 pp. MF-01; PC-01.

"Enrollment Managers Warned: Several Skills Required to Navigate the Future." December 1997. *Enrollment Management Report* 1(9): 1+.

Ewers, P., and A. Kennedy. 1984. "Leadership for Enrollment Management: The Next Phase." Paper presented at a College Board conference, Organizing for Enrollment Management. Chicago: College Board.

Glassner, William A. Summer 1993. "Tapping a Hidden Source of Financial Aid." *College Board Review* 168: 2–8.

Graff, A.S. 1986. "Organizing the Resources." In *Managing College Enrollments,* edited by D. Hossler. New Directions for Higher Education No. 53. San Francisco: Jossey-Bass.

Greene, E. 18 February 1987. "Colleges Turn to 'Enrollment Management' as a Way to Attract and Keep Better Students." *Chronicle of Higher Education:* 27–29.

Grove, Josephine. 1992. "The Marketing Aspect of Enrollment Management: Evaluating the Impact on Recruitment and Retention in Institutions of Higher Education." Master's thesis, Fontbonne College. ED 354 929. 143 pp. MF-01; PC-06.

Gunn, Mary, and Richard Backes. Spring 1992. "Avoidance of Papin: The Registrar's Role in Enrollment Management." *College and University* 67(3): 183–86.

Hartle, T.W. Summer 1994. "The Battle over Governmental Regulation of Academe." *College Board Review* 172: 14–21+.

Healy, P., and P. Schmidt. 10 January 1997. "Public Colleges Expect Tough Competition in Annual Fight for State Appropriations." *Chronicle of Higher Education:* A29+.

Hilpert, J., and R. Alfred. Summer 1987. "Improving Enrollment Success: Presidents Hold the Key." *Educational Record* 68(3): 30–35.

Hodgkinson, H.L. March/April 1983. "Guess Who's Coming to College." *Academe:* 13–19.

———. June 1985. "All One System." *Demographics of Education, Kindergarten through Graduate School.* Washington, D.C.: Institute for Educational Leadership.

Hossler, D. 1984. *Enrollment Management: An Integrated Approach.* New York: College Board. ED 249 906. 174 pp. MF-01; PC not available EDRS.

———. 1986. *Creating Effective Enrollment Management Systems.* New York: College Board.

———. Winter 1987a. "Enrollment Management: Institutional Applications." *College and University* 62(2): 106–16.

———. July 1987b. "Enrollment Planning: A New Iteration of the Planning Process." Paper presented at a College Board conference, Enrollment Management: The Next Step. Chicago: College Board and Indiana University.

———. 1991. *Evaluating Student Recruitment and Retention Programs.* New Directions for Institutional Research No. 70. San Francisco: Jossey-Bass.

Hossler, D., J.P. Bean, and Associates, eds. 1990. *The Strategic Management of College Enrollments.* San Francisco: Jossey-Bass.

Hossler, D., and F.R. Kemerer. 1986. "Enrollment Management and Its Context." In *Managing College Enrollments,* edited by D. Hossler. New Directions for Higher Education No. 53. San Francisco: Jossey-Bass.

Ingersoll, R.J. 1988. *The Enrollment Problem.* New York: American Council on Education.

Ingersoll, Williams, and Associates. February 1992. "Fall 1991 National Enrollment Management Survey Report." Littleton, Colo.: Noel-Levitz Center for Enrollment Management.

Johnson, A.B., and C.F. Thompson. 1992. "Data-Based Enrollment Management." *College Student Journal* 26(1): 140–44.

Jump, James W. Spring 1995. "The Ethics of Need-Blind Admission." *Journal of College Admission* 147: 12–15.

Kajcienski, Don. Spring 1996. "Admission Recruiters and Territory Management: Some Lessons from Business." *Journal of College Admission* 151: 24–30.

Keller, G. 1984. "Strategic Planning: Linking Enrollment to Institutional Priorities." Paper presented at a meeting of the College Board, July, Chicago, Illinois.

Kemerer, F.R. Winter 1984–85. "The Role of Deans, Department Chairs, and Faculty in Enrollment Management." *College Board Review* 134: 4–8+.

Kemerer, F.R., J.V. Baldridge, and K.C. Green. 1982. *Strategies for Effective Enrollment Management.* Washington, D.C.: American Association of State Colleges and Universities.

Kemerer, F.R., and T. Huddleston. 1984. "The Organizational Aspects of Enrollment Management: Theory and Practice." Paper presented at a College Board conference, Leadership for Enrollment Management. Chicago: University of Chicago–Loyola, College Board.

Kreutner, L., and E.S. Godfrey. Winter 1980–81. "Enrollment Management: A New Vehicle for Institutional Renewal." *College Board Review* 118: 6–9+.

Krotsen, Marsha V. Spring 1992. "Case Study: "Using Enrollment Management to Enhance Quality at the University of Hartford." *College and University* 67(3): 173–82.

———. 1993. "Designing Executive Information Systems for Enrollment Management." In *Developing Executive Information Systems for Higher Education,* edited by Robert H. Glover and Marsha V. Krotzen. New Directions for Institutional Research No. 77. San Francisco: Jossey-Bass.

Lembecke, Barbara A. 1994. "Organizational Performance Measures: The Vital Signs of TQM Investments." In *Total Quality Management on Campus: Is It Worth Doing?* edited by Daniel Seymour. New Directions for Higher Education No. 86. San Francisco: Jossey-Bass.

Levine, A. 31 January 1997. "Higher Education's New Status as a Mature Industry." *Chronicle of Higher Education:* A48.

Lewis, S.R. Spring 1995. "Ensuring Access, Strengthening Institutions." *College Board Review* 175: 12–17.

McDonough, Patricia M. July/August 1994. "Buying and Selling Higher Education: The Social Construction of the College Applicant." *Journal of Higher Education* 65(4): 427–46.

McDonough, Patricia M., and Larry Robertson. Spring 1995. "Reclaiming the Educational Role of Chief Admission Officers." *Journal of College Admission* 147: 22–31.

McGowan, R. Spring 1996. "Open Forum. It's What You Know for Sure: Using Evaluation to Improve Performance." *Journal of College Admission* 151: 4–5.

McPherson, M.S., and M.O. Schapiro. Spring 1995. "Pricing and

Financial Aid in a Shifting Environment." *College Board Review* 175: 18–21.

Mahoney, J.L. 1996. "The Crisis of Respectability." *Journal of College Admission* 150: 3–5.

Mendoza, Jose, and Miguel Corzo. 1996. "Tracking/Monitoring Program to Enhance Multicultural Student Retention." Paper presented at the Eighth Annual Summer Institute of the Consortium for Community College Development, June, Charleston, South Carolina. ED 399 999. 24 pp. MF-01; PC-01.

Merante, J.A. Fall 1987. "Organizing to Manage Enrollment." *College Board Review* 145: 14–17+.

Moss, Ron W. Fall 1995. "A Generation of Variance: Are We Prepared?" *Journal of College Admission* 149: 18–22.

Moyer, Richard A. 1996. "Strategies for Increasing Enrollment and WSCH during a Period of Downsizing." Paper presented at the 21st Annual Conference of the Association of California Community College Administrators, March 14, Costa Mesa, California. ED 395 612. 7 pp. MF-01; PC-01.

Murray, D. 1986. "A Case Study: DePauw University." In *Creating Effective Management Systems,* edited by D. Hossler. New York: College Entrance Examination Board.

National Association of College Admission Counselors. August 1990. "Admission Trends 1990: A Survey of NACAC Member Colleges and Universities." *NACAC Bulletin.* Washington, D.C.: Author.

Neuner, Jerome L. Fall 1992. "1992 AAUA Exemplary Models and John L. Blackburn Awards. Doing More with Less: The Challenge of Constraints." *Journal of Higher Education Management* 8(1): 3–5.

Noel-Levitz National Center for Enrollment Management. 1996. *Fall 1995 National Enrollment Management Survey. Executive Summary of Findings: Four-Year Colleges and Universities.* Littleton, Colo.: Author.

Noya, R. Spring 1997. "Financial Leveraging in Higher Education: How Is It Done, Does It Work, Is It Fair, and What Is Its Role in the 90s?" *On Target: Recruiting and Enrollment Strategies for 2000 and Beyond* 25: 19–23.

O'Brien, Ed, et al. 1995. *A Review of Enrollment Management: Issues and Strategies.* Management/Marketing Special Project. Phoenix: Maricopa County Community College District. ED 381 184. 160 pp. MF-01; PC-07.

Ohio Board of Regents. 1996. *The Challenge Is Change: 1996 Master Plan.* Columbus: Author.

Pollock, C.R. 1987a. "Enrollment Management: No Little Plan for the Future of Student Affairs." *Enrollment Management: The*

Next Step. Chicago: College Board and Indiana University.

————. 1987b. "Enrollment Management Structures and Activities at Four-Year Institutions of Higher Education." Doctoral dissertation, Univ. of Massachusetts.

Porter, O.F. August 1990. "Demographics and Decline in the 1990s: Threat or Menace?" *NACAC Bulletin:* 17–24.

Rentz, Audrey L., et al. 1996. *Student Affairs Practice in Higher Education*. 2d ed. Springfield, Ill.: Charles C. Thomas.

Richter, B., ed. *n.d.* "Quality Service: A Driving Force for Colleges Today." Mimeographed. Coralville, Ia.: USA Group/Noel-Levitz Centers for Institutional Effectiveness and Innovation.

Sampson, Cedric A., et al. 1995. "Vision 2000: A Strategic Plan for College of the Redwoods." Eureka, Calif.: College of the Redwoods. ED 396 805. 43 pp. MF-01; PC-02.

Sanjeev, Arun P., and Jan M. Zytkow. 1995. "Automated Knowledge Discovery in Institutional Data to Support Enrollment Management." Paper presented at the 35th Annual Forum of the Association for Institutional Research, May, Boston, Massachusetts. ED 387 017. 24 pp. MF-01; PC-01.

Sanoff, A.P. 26 September 1994. "Admissions Deans on the Hot Seat." *US News & World Report* 117(12): 98–100.

Seidman, Alan. 1995. "Parkland College Enrollment Management Model." Champaign, Ill.: Parkland College. ED 384 375. 23 pp. MF-01; PC-01.

Sevier, R. Summer 1992. "Is Demography Destiny?" *Journal of College Admission* 135: 13–22.

Seymour, D. 1992. "TQM on Campus." *AAHE Bulletin* 44(37): 10–13+.

————. January/February 1994. "The Baldrige Cometh." *Change* 26(1): 16–27.

Shafer, B.S., and L.E. Coate. November 1992. "Benchmarking in Higher Education." *NACUBO Business Officer:* 28–35.

Sidle, Margaret Wright. 1995. "Enrollment Management: Do Resource Allocation Decisions Really Make a Difference?" Paper presented at the 20th Annual Meeting of the Association for the Study of Higher Education, November, Orlando, Florida. ED 391 433. 32 pp. MF-01; PC-02.

Snider, T. 1984. "One Short Step for Directors of Admission." Paper presented at a meeting of the College Board, July, Chicago, Illinois.

————. 1987. "Management Information Systems: Its Role in the Enrollment Management Model." Paper presented at a meeting of the College Board, June/July, New Orleans, Louisiana, and Evanston, Illinois.

Snyder, T. 1987. *Digest of Education Statistics, 1987.* Washington, D.C.: National Center for Education Statistics. ED 282 359. 424 pp. MF-01; PC-17.

Snyder, T., and C.M. Hoffman. 1995. *Digest of Education Statistics, 1995.* Washington, D.C.: National Center for Education Statistics. ED 387 885. 604 pp. MF-03; PC-25.

Speck, Samuel W. March/April 1996. "Tuition: How We Made the Cut." *Trusteeship* 4(2): 6–10.

Swanson, Roger M., and Christine Kajikawa Wilkinson. 1993. *Training New Admissions Recruiters: A Guide for Survival and Success.* Washington, D.C.: Council for Advancement and Support of Education. ED 362 128. 87 pp. MF-01; PC not available EDRS.

Townsley, Michael K. Winter/Spring 1993. "A Strategic Model for Enrollment-Driven Private Colleges." *Journal for Higher Education Management* 8(2): 57–66.

Trachtenberg, Stephen J. 21 March 1997. "Preparing for Baby Boomers: Older Students Will Bring New Opportunities to Colleges." *Chronicle of Higher Education:* B7.

U.S. House of Representatives, Committee on Economic and Educational Opportunities, Subcommittee on Postsecondary Education, Training, and Life-Long Learning. 23 April 1996. "Who Plays, Who Pays, Who Goes?" Hearing on higher education. 104th Congress, Second Session. Serial No. 104-55. ED 399 902. 124 pp. MF-01; PC-05.

Wallenfeldt, E.C. 1983. *American Higher Education.* Westport, Conn.: Greenwood Press.

Weissman, Julie, and Jane Stroupe. 1993. "Enrollment Projections: Combining Statistics and Gut Feelings." Paper presented at the 33rd Annual Forum of the Association for Institutional Research, May, Chicago, Illinois. ED 360 907. 13 pp. MF-01; PC-01.

Western Interstate Commission for Higher Education. 1988. *High School Graduates: Projections by State, 1986–2004.* Boulder, Colo.: WICHE, TIAA, and the College Board. ED 296 676. 61 pp. MF-01; PC-03.

———. 1993. *High School Graduates: Projections by State, 1992–2009.* Boulder, Colo.: WICHE, TIAA, and the College Board.

Wharton, J.C.R. March 1983. "Enrollment: Higher Education's Window of Vulnerability." *Change:* 20–22.

Wiese, Michael D. 1994. "College Choice Cognitive Dissonance: Managing Student/Institution Fit." *Journal of Marketing for Higher Education* 5(1): 35–47.

INDEX

A

access to higher education, 4
accountability, 4
age as a factor in college enrollments, 11–13
American Association of Collegiate Registrars and Admissions
    Officers, 20
Arizona State University, 34–35

C

California State University at Los Angeles, 41
committee model of enrollment management, 17–18
communicating results, 44
coordinator model of enrollment management, 17–18
cost of education, 5
credibility of higher education, 49
current enrollment management practices in public universities,
    43–45

D

definitions, 15–16, 43
demographic factors, 11–14
discounting tuition, 54
division model of enrollment management, 17–18
Dolence study of enrollment management, 25
dwindling financial support, 4–5
dwindling political support, 4–5

E

East Tennessee State University, 39–40
enrollment management
        committee, 17–18
        continuum, 20
        definitions, 15–16, 43
        goals of, 15
        idea system, 21–22
        key elements of, 43
        models of, 17–19
        structure for, 43
ethical dilemmas, 53–55
ethics, 45
evaluation, 44

F

faculty, role of, 51–53
federal
        aid, 6–7

public institutions, 3
public opinion, 3
public perception, 9–11
public universities, 27–45

Q
quality, evaluation of, 50–51

R
regulations, 6–9
       federal, 6–9
       state, 4
Richter, 52

S
Shafer and Coate, 15
Snyder, 12
societal changes, 13
Speck, 10
state
       appropriations, 5
       institutions, 3
       issues, 4–6
       regulations, 4–6
       support, 4–6
structure, 43–44, 47–48
survey, business officers, 15
survey, organizational, 23

T
tuition, 10

U
U.S. Department of Education, financial aid, 7
University of Arizona, 35–37
University of Central Florida, 38–39
University of Connecticut, 29–30
University of Maine, 28
University of Memphis, 40–41

V
value of higher education, 49

ASHE-ERIC HIGHER EDUCATION REPORTS

Since 1983, the Association for the Study of Higher Education (ASHE) and the Educational Resources Information Center (ERIC) Clearinghouse on Higher Education, a sponsored project of the Graduate School of Education and Human Development at The George Washington University, have cosponsored the ASHE-ERIC Higher Education Report series. This volume is the twenty-sixth overall and the ninth to be published by the Graduate School of Education and Human Development at The George Washington University.

Each monograph is the definitive analysis of a tough higher education problem, based on thorough research of pertinent literature and institutional experiences. Topics are identified by a national survey. Noted practitioners and scholars are then commissioned to write the reports, with experts providing critical reviews of each manuscript before publication.

Eight monographs (10 before 1985) in the ASHE-ERIC Higher Education Report series are published each year and are available on individual and subscription bases. To order, use the order form on the last page of this book.

Qualified persons interested in writing a monograph for the ASHE-ERIC Higher Education Report series are invited to submit a proposal to the National Advisory Board. As the preeminent literature review and issue analysis series in higher education, the Higher Education Reports are guaranteed wide dissemination and national exposure for accepted candidates. Execution of a monograph requires at least a minimal familiarity with the ERIC database, including *Resources in Education* and the current *Index to Journals in Education.* The objective of these reports is to bridge conventional wisdom with practical research. Prospective authors are strongly encouraged to call at (800) 773-3742 ext. 14.

For further information, write to
    ASHE-ERIC Higher Education Report Series
    The George Washington University
    One Dupont Circle, Suite 630
    Washington, DC 20036-1183
Or phone (202) 296-2597
Toll free: (800) 773-ERIC

Write or call for a complete catalog.

Visit our Web site at **www.eriche.org**

ADVISORY BOARD

James Earl Davis
University of Delaware at Newark

Kenneth A. Feldman
State University of New York–Stony Brook

Kassie Freeman
Peabody College, Vanderbilt University

Susan Frost
Emory University

Esther E. Gottlieb
West Virginia University

Philo Hutcheson
Georgia State University

Lori White
Stanford University

CONSULTING EDITORS

Thomas A. Angelo
University of Miami

Sandra Beyer
University of Texas at El Paso

Robert Boice
State University of New York–Stony Brook

Ivy E. Broder
The American University

Dennis Brown
Michigan State University

Shirley M. Clark
Oregon State System of Higher Education

Robert A. Cornesky
Cornesky and Associates, Inc.

K. Patricia Cross
Scholar in Residence

Rhonda Martin Epper
State Higher Education Executive Officers

Cheryl Falk
Yakima Valley Community College

Anne H. Frank
American Association of University Professors

Mildred Garcia
Arizona State University–West

Don Hossler
Indiana University

Dean L. Hubbard
Northwest Missouri State University

Lisa R. Lattuca
The Spencer Foundation, Chicago, Illinois

J. Roderick Lauver
Planned Systems International, Inc.–Maryland

Daniel T. Layzell
MGT of America, Inc., Madison, Wisconsin

Barbara Lee
Rutgers University

Ivan B. Liss
Radford University

Anne Goodsell Love
University of Akron

Clara M. Lovett
Northern Arizona University

Meredith Ludwig
Education Statistics Services Institute

Jean MacGregor
Evergreen State College

William McKeachie
University of Michigan

Laurence R. Marcus
Rowan College

Mantha V. Mehallis
Florida Atlantic University

Robert Menges
Northwestern University

Diane E. Morrison
Centre for Curriculum, Transfer, and Technology

John A. Muffo
Virginia Polytechnic Institute and State University

Patricia H. Murrell
University of Memphis

L. Jackson Newell
Deep Springs College

Steven G. Olswang
University of Washington

R. Eugene Rice
American Association for Higher Education

Sherry Sayles-Folks
Eastern Michigan University

Maria Scatena
St. Mary of the Woods College

John Schuh
Iowa State University

Jack H. Schuster
Claremont Graduate School–Center for Educational Studies

Carole Schwinn
Jackson Community College

Patricia Somers
University of Arkansas at Little Rock

Leonard Springer
University of Wisconsin–Madison

Marilla D. Svinicki
University of Texas–Austin

David Sweet
OERI, U.S. Department of Education

Jon E. Travis
Texas A&M University

Dan W. Wheeler
University of Nebraska–Lincoln

Christine K. Wilkinson
Arizona State University

Donald H. Wulff
University of Washington

Manta Yorke
Liverpool John Moores University

William Zeller
University of Michigan at Ann Arbor

REVIEW PANEL

Richard Alfred
University of Michigan

Robert J. Barak
Iowa State Board of Regents

Alan Bayer
Virginia Polytechnic Institute and State University

John P. Bean
Indiana University–Bloomington

John M. Braxton
Peabody College, Vanderbilt University

Ellen M. Brier
Tennessee State University

Dennis Brown
University of Kansas

Patricia Carter
University of Michigan

John A. Centra
Syracuse University

Paul B. Chewning
Council for the Advancement and Support of Education

Arthur W. Chickering
Vermont College

Darrel A. Clowes
Virginia Polytechnic Institute and State University

Deborah M. DiCroce
Piedmont Virginia Community College

Dorothy E. Finnegan
The College of William & Mary

Kenneth C. Green
Claremont Graduate University

James C. Hearn
University of Georgia

Edward R. Hines
Illinois State University

Deborah Hunter
University of Vermont

Linda K. Johnsrud
University of Hawaii at Manoa

Bruce Anthony Jones
University of Missouri–Columbia

Elizabeth A. Jones
West Virginia University

Marsha V. Krotseng
State College and University Systems of West Virginia

George D. Kuh
Indiana University–Bloomington

J. Roderick Lauver
Planned Systems International, Inc.–Maryland

Daniel T. Layzell
MGT of America, Inc., Madison, Wisconsin

Patrick G. Love
Kent State University

Meredith Jane Ludwig
American Association of State Colleges and Universities

Mantha V. Mehallis
Florida Atlantic University

Toby Milton
Essex Community College

John A. Muffo
Virginia Polytechnic Institute and State University

L. Jackson Newell
Deep Springs College

Mark Oromaner
Hudson Community College

James C. Palmer
Illinois State University

Robert A. Rhoads
Michigan State University

G. Jeremiah Ryan
Quincy College

Mary Ann Danowitz Sagaria
The Ohio State University

Kathryn Nemeth Tuttle
University of Kansas

Volume 26 ASHE-ERIC Higher Education Reports

1. Faculty Workload Studies: Perspectives, Needs, and Future Directions
   Katrina A. Meyer

2. Assessing Faculty Publication Productivity: Issues of Equity
   Elizabeth G. Creamer

3. Proclaiming and Sustaining Excellence: Assessment as a Faculty Role
   Karen Maitland Schilling and Karl L. Schilling

4. Creating Learning Centered Classrooms: What Does Learning Theory Have to Say?
   Frances K. Stage, Patricia A. Muller, Jillian Kinzie, and Ada Simmons

5. The Academic Administrator and the Law: What Every Dean and Department Chair Needs to Know
   J. Douglas Toma and Richard L. Palm

6. The Powerful Potential of Learning Communities: Improving Education for the Future
   Oscar T. Lenning and Larry H. Ebbers

Volume 25 ASHE-ERIC Higher Education Reports

1. A Culture for Academic Excellence: Implementing the Quality Principles in Higher Education
   Jann E. Freed, Marie R. Klugman, and Jonathan D. Fife

2. From Discipline to Development: Rethinking Student Conduct in Higher Education
   Michael Dannells

3. Academic Controversy: Enriching College Instruction through Intellectual Conflict
   David W. Johnson, Roger T. Johnson, and Karl A. Smith

4. Higher Education Leadership: Analyzing the Gender Gap
   Luba Chliwniak

5. The Virtual Campus: Technology and Reform in Higher Education
   Gerald C. Van Dusen

6. Early Intervention Programs: Opening the Door to Higher Education
   Robert H. Fenske, Christine A. Geranios, Jonathan E. Keller, and David E. Moore

7. The Vitality of Senior Faculty Members: Snow on the Roof— Fire in the Furnace
   Carole J. Bland and William H. Bergquist

8. A National Review of Scholastic Achievement in General Education: How Are We Doing and Why Should We Care?
   Steven J. Osterlind

Volume 24 ASHE-ERIC Higher Education Reports

1. Tenure, Promotion, and Reappointment: Legal and Administrative Implications
   Benjamin Baez and John A. Centra

2. Taking Teaching Seriously: Meeting the Challenge of Instructional Improvement
   Michael B. Paulsen and Kenneth A. Feldman

3. Empowering the Faculty: Mentoring Redirected and Renewed
   Gaye Luna and Deborah L. Cullen

4. Enhancing Student Learning: Intellectual, Social, and Emotional Integration
   Anne Goodsell Love and Patrick G. Love

5. Benchmarking in Higher Education: Adapting Best Practices to Improve Quality
   Jeffrey W. Alstete

6. Models for Improving College Teaching: A Faculty Resource
   Jon E. Travis

7. Experiential Learning in Higher Education: Linking Classroom and Community
   Jeffrey A. Cantor

8. Successful Faculty Development and Evaluation: The Complete Teaching Portfolio
   John P. Murray

Volume 23 ASHE-ERIC Higher Education Reports

1. The Advisory Committee Advantage: Creating an Effective Strategy for Programmatic Improvement
   Lee Teitel

2. Collaborative Peer Review: The Role of Faculty in Improving College Teaching
   Larry Keig and Michael D. Waggoner

3. Prices, Productivity, and Investment: Assessing Financial Strategies in Higher Education
   Edward P. St. John

4. The Development Officer in Higher Education: Toward an Understanding of the Role
   Michael J. Worth and James W. Asp II

5. Measuring Up: The Promises and Pitfalls of Performance Indicators in Higher Education
   Gerald Gaither, Brian P. Nedwek, and John E. Neal

6. A New Alliance: Continuous Quality and Classroom Effectiveness
   Mimi Wolverton

7. Redesigning Higher Education: Producing Dramatic Gains in Student Learning
   Lion F. Gardiner

8. Student Learning outside the Classroom: Transcending Artificial Boundaries
   George D. Kuh, Katie Branch Douglas, Jon P. Lund, and Jackie Ramin-Gyurnek

Volume 22 ASHE-ERIC Higher Education Reports

1. The Department Chair: New Roles, Responsibilities, and Challenges
   Alan T. Seagren, John W. Creswell, and Daniel W. Wheeler

2. Sexual Harassment in Higher Education: From Conflict to Community
   Robert O. Riggs, Patricia H. Murrell, and JoAnne C. Cutting

3. Chicanos in Higher Education: Issues and Dilemmas for the 21st Century
   Adalberto Aguirre, Jr., and Ruben O. Martinez

4. Academic Freedom in American Higher Education: Rights, Responsibilities, and Limitations
   Robert K. Poch

5. Making Sense of the Dollars: The Costs and Uses of Faculty Compensation
   Kathryn M. Moore and Marilyn J. Amey

6. Enhancing Promotion, Tenure, and Beyond: Faculty Socialization as a Cultural Process
   William G. Tierney and Robert A. Rhoads

7. New Perspectives for Student Affairs Professionals: Evolving Realities, Responsibilities, and Roles
   Peter H. Garland and Thomas W. Grace

8. Turning Teaching into Learning: The Role of Student Responsibility in the Collegiate Experience
   Todd M. Davis and Patricia Hillman Murrell

Quantity   **Amount**

_____ Please begin my subscription to the current year's
ASHE-ERIC Higher Education Reports at $144.00, 25%
off the cover price, starting with Report 1.   _____

_____ Please send a complete set of Volume 27 (Year 2000)
ASHE-ERIC Higher Education Reports at $144.00, over
25% off the cover price.   _____

Individual reports are available for $24.00 and include the cost of shipping and handling.

SECURE ON-LINE ORDERING
is now available on our web site.
www.eriche.org/reports

SHIPPING POLICY:

• Books are sent UPS Ground or equivalent. For faster delivery, call for
charges. Alaska, Hawaii, U.S. Territories, and Foreign Countries, please
call for shipping information. Order will be shipped within 24 hours
after receipt of request. Orders of 10 or more books, call for shipping
information. All prices shown are subject to change.

• Returns: No cash refunds—credit will be applied to future orders.

PLEASE SEND ME THE FOLLOWING REPORTS:

Quantity	Volume/No.	Title	Amount

Please check one of the following:

☐ Check enclosed, payable to GW-ERIC.

☐ Purchase order attached.

☐ Charge my credit card indicated below:
  ☐ Visa   ☐ MasterCard

| | | | | | | | | | | | | | | | |

Expiration Date_____

Subtotal: _____

Less Discount: _____

Total Due: _____

Name_____

Title _____ E-mail _____

Institution _____

Address_____

City _____ State _____ Zip_____

Phone _____ Fax _____Telex_____

Signature_____ Date_____

SEND ALL ORDERS TO:

ASHE-ERIC Higher Education Reports Series
One Dupont Cir., Ste. 630, Washington, DC 20036-1183
Phone: (202) 296-2597 ext. 13 Toll-free: (800) 773-ERIC ext. 13
FAX: (202) 452-1844
EMAIL: order@eric-he.edu
Secure on-line ordering at URL: www.eriche.org/reports

**Secure on-line ordering
is available:
visit our web site at
www.eriche.org/reports**